PTA Fundraising
Fundraising ideas and tips for anyone involved in their PTA

Anne Dunn

ISBN-13: 978-1532745409

ISBN-10: 1532745400

CONTENTS

Introduction

The aim of this book is to assist anyone involved in their PTA, whether they have just joined or if they have been involved for a while but are looking for new ideas or tips. The book gives an overview of what a PTA is and what it does. PTAs are very diverse, with some for tiny schools with 60 children all the way up to PTAs for big schools with 2000 children. But they all have one thing in common- wanting to raise money for their schools to help improve the experience of children at their school.

A wide selection of fundraising ideas are included, with each one being clearly explained. There is a section of "must do" fundraising ideas- "must do" because they can raise significant amounts of money with minimal effort from the PTA. Other sections of the book give information on Big Events which are more complex but potentially high earners.

The book includes sample fliers, letters and action sheets. There are sections on communicating with parents to try to improve engagement with parents as well as the importance of the PTA and School working well together.

There is also a section for Treasurers with a few tips to try to help make their job easier so they can concentrate on fundraising!

Although this book is written primarily with PTAs in mind, many of the fundraising ideas and other principles can apply to other organisations who wish to fundraise for a good cause. The book is written in England, so much of the legal information only applies there, however the ideas and templates should be useful for PTAs and other organisations wherever they are located.

Anne Dunn

1 ABOUT PTAS

What is a PTA?

PTA stands for Parent Teacher Association. All parents of children at a school (and other carers) are members, together with all staff at the school. Traditionally, the PTA of a school will fundraise in order to purchase items or pay for other things that will enrich and improve the school experience for the pupils of the school. PTAs will often run events as fundraising exercises, but can also run events for the children and wider community for other reasons such as to provide the children with a new experience or to foster community spirit.

PTAs are run by a Committee. They will have certain key Committee positions which will always include the Chair, Secretary and Treasurer and can also include others such as Vice Chair, Events Co-Ordinator, Marketing Co-Ordinator or any other position that the PTA feels is necessary and that they can appoint to. However they rely on the support from volunteers - whether by attending meetings to help decide how the PTA should fundraise, or by helping out with events. Even helping out at one event a year is valuable help for the PTA.

Most schools have PTAs. They all work hard to raise money and any amount raised benefits the children. It is up to the PTA to decide how to spend the money they raise. Usually the school will make suggestions about what the PTA could purchase, however the final decision on what the money is spent on is that of the PTA.

PTAs are not just about the money though as they can boost the feeling of community within the school- for example by running social events at a breakeven or subsidised cost for the good of the school. PTAs can also benefit the wider community depending on the events raised and the degree of local involvement / support.

Being involved with your school's PTA can be very rewarding- it can mean that you get to know other parents at the school that you may not otherwise have come into contact with, and you may make lifelong friends. You can gain new skills and experience which can be satisfying on a personal level that could also help with your career- being able to say at application and at interview that I had been Treasurer for the PTA for a number of years was what made one interview panel offer a job to me over the other candidates for the role. Knowing that you have helped make a difference to the children at the school by helping fundraise for something that will enrich their school experience is immensely satisfying. Being involved with the PTA can be hard work, but most PTA members will say that the satisfaction they get from their involvement is worth the work that they put in.

2 REASONS TO FUNDRAISE

The most obvious reason to fundraise is of course to get money for the PTA to spend on the school. In these days of ever increasing pressures on school finances, the contribution the PTA can make to help finance things to improve the school and learning experience for the children is increasingly valuable to schools. The school can request that the PTA purchase particular items or contribute towards a larger project.

PTAs should remember that the decision on what to spend the money they raise is theirs rather than that of the school. Some PTAs have very clear definitions of what they will or won't contribute towards financially, others are happy for the school to make suggestions that the PTA will decide on individually. Many schools come to the PTA with a "wishlist" at the start of the academic year which the PTA can consider and make a decision on which of the items on the wishlist they are happy to fundraise for.

The other reason to fundraise is to build community spirit for the school pupils, families and wider communities. Large social events give opportunities to invite the wider community and extended families which is good for the school's place in the local community. Fundraising events can teach children (and parents) new skills in terms of team working, organisation and working towards a common goal.

The PTA can make a big difference to the children at the school both in terms of what they contribute to financially but also the events that they run. Many PTAs run events that are designed to raise money, but also will run some at "break even" costs which are more about the event for the children and school than to make money. Remember that the reason the PTA is fundraising is to improve the learning and school experience for the children so although fundraising helps with this because it means they can contribute financially, it can be just as valuable to the children if the PTA runs events that they may not otherwise get to experience. Some children have real deprivation at home and a PTA run trip to the pantomime might be their only opportunity to experience a trip to the theatre, or the PTA running a book swap event might be one of the few chances a child has to choose their own books for themselves. It's great to make money but don't lose sight of the reason why the PTA is raising money i.e. to benefit the children so if it is possible to run some events along the way that directly benefit the children as well as the pure fundraising events that can only be a good thing and can be as satisfying to PTA members as raising lots of money at a big event.

3 PARENTS

Parents are a vital part of your PTA! For a PTA to be successful, it needs to have as many parents on board as possible. Not just with attending meetings but helping at events or even just supporting PTA activities by participating in them with their child whether that is by purchasing cakes at the cake stall or helping their child enter competitions the PTA might be running.

Parents should be welcomed and encouraged to be involved in their PTA. Everyone has different jobs and demands on their time so some parents will have less ability to be involved than others but any contribution they can make is a valuable one- even if it is helping out at one event a year. Getting sufficient parent engagement is a challenge most PTAs will have. There is a separate chapter on ways to improve engagement however the key thing that any PTA can do is to make sure they appear approachable and not a "closed shop" or "clique" as this will deter many parents who could be persuaded to help out. Good communication is key to achieving this.

The parent population at school is a treasure trove of potential skills that could be valuable to the PTA. Parents will come from a diverse range of backgrounds and have a diverse range of jobs. It can be a very useful exercise to do a skills audit of parents every year (one large one if this is the first time the PTA is doing it and then one for the parents of the new children annually after that). You could do this as part of a wider information seeking exercise from parents that although may take some time to collate the responses will be a worthwhile investment in terms of the information that you gain from it. Then you will know if you have an advanced cake maker that you can approach to see if they might be willing to make a "show stopper" cake or someone who is really good at marketing that might be able to help promote a big event.

4 SCHOOL

This might seem obvious- the PTA is the Parent Teacher Association and it raises money for the school. It is important to have a good relationship with the school- they can provide invaluable support to the PTA which in turn allows the PTA to raise more money. Many PTAs have an excellent relationship with their school.

Ways that the school can support the PTA

The school can support the PTA in almost infinite ways, but here are some examples:

- A staff member running a crèche during PTA meetings for pupils and younger siblings of the parents attending the PTA meeting.
- Letting the PTA use the school photocopier to copy fliers / newsletters to distribute in the weekly information bag. Sometimes if you're lucky they might even offer to copy the flier for you!
- Allowing a non-uniform day- either to raise money or for the children to bring in an item each for use as prizes at a future event
- Supporting events such as a Mothers Day shop by letting the children out of class to choose their presents and write the gift cards (or even better getting them to write their gift cards in class)
- Letting children do pictures for a PTA competition in class time (for example a competition to decide which picture will be a calendar / cd cover)
- Always sending a School Representative to the PTA meetings. Ideally someone who can make decisions there and then so the Headteacher is the best person but if they cannot attend another School Representative

is still useful even if they cannot agree everything straight away.

- Letting the PTA run School Discos after school, particularly ones that go on later than the staff would normally be staying until. Many schools have a policy that if a Disco is on the staff will stay and help manage it so this is a big effort for all the staff.
- Helping out with events at the school whether Discos, Cake Stalls, talent shows, displaying things that the PTA is trying to sell.
- Letting children do their Christmas card / tea towel etc. picture designs in school time.
- Putting the PTA fliers into the weekly information bags rather than getting a PTA member to do it.
- Sending texts out to parents on the school text system for PTA purposes.
- Collecting the money that is sent in by parents for PTA events / fundraising schemes. Sometimes they will count it for you and do a list of who has / hasn't paid.
- Coming to PTA events held outside school time – at evenings or weekends. School staff work hard and long enough hours as it is, so to come and support a PTA event in their time off should really be appreciated, particularly if they don't live locally or have young children themselves. Interestingly, whilst researching for this book, some of the teachers I spoke to said that they really valued their PTA and coming to help out at the two annual fairs was really worthwhile to them because of the benefits they saw from what the PTA contributed to the school.
- Letting the PTA sell raffle tickets at school events such as school performances and having the raffle draw as part of that event.

- Letting the PTA run other big events at the School, usually outside normal school time- such as Promise Auctions, Summer Fairs, Christmas Fairs etc.
- Allowing a PTA member to come to the induction evening for the parents of the next intake of children (ie Reception / Year 7) and talk to them about the PTA.
- Allowing PTA members to give presentations in assemblies that parents are invited to- whether to show them how to use a fundraising website or to inform or consult on other issues.

As the school environment becomes more stressful to staff due to budget cuts and work demands, staff in some schools may struggle to find the time to support their PTA. Because of the budget cuts, the contribution that the PTA can make in terms of buying "extras" for the children is even more valuable than before. But as staff at schools come under more pressure at work they may be less keen to support the PTA. If your school is less positive or supportive to the PTA than you feel they should be, you could try some of the following tips:

- Try to identify why the school is less positive or supportive than you might hope-
    - Is it a new PTA that is just starting up?
    - Is it an existing PTA but with different committee members? (and if so were there any issues between the previous committee and the school that are making the school reluctant to support the PTA now?)
    - Has the school historically not been involved with the PTA?
    - Is the school just too busy with its core work and feels it cannot support the PTA?

If relationships between the PTA and the school aren't as positive as they could be, consider requesting a meeting between one or two PTA Committee members and a member of the school staff. Explain that you want to raise money for the school and try to identify the things that the PTA can do to help the school. Examples of how the PTA can help support the school are below:

- Fundraising to purchase things that benefit the children as "extras" but that also benefit the school and its individual teachers by enriching and enhancing the learning experience of the children. Possible examples could be:
  - New books (to help with attainment in reading)
  - Smart boards (most schools have these now but many PTAs were involved in purchasing these for schools when they were new so this is a good example of how the PTA can help support a school in purchasing something that really helps the school)
  - Outdoor furniture- to allow the children to spend more time outside
  - Forest school equipment- Forest school is becoming more popular but it does need some equipment to be purchased, could the PTA help if this is something the school wants to do
  - iPads- again many schools have these now, but when they first started to become popular in schools many PTAs helped fund them. If school uses iPads, could it use more? Having them to share is great but the learning experience of the children sharing equipment is different to the more

active learning experience they will get if they can use one each- this goes for all sorts of equipment not just iPads.

- o Has the school got a current PTA "wishlist" of things that they would like the PTA to fundraise for? Is there equipment that the school needs that would benefit pupils but would also benefit the school in terms of helping the teachers or school staff either with day to day things or by helping the children with their learning? If there isn't a current "wishlist" ask the School to make one for the next PTA meeting so that it can be considered.

5 LEGAL CONSIDERATIONS

Constitution

PTAs should have a Constitution which is a set of rules which sets out how the PTA will be run. The Constitution will specify the Committee positions which will run the PTA together with details about how the meetings will be run, how many Committee members need to be present at a meeting for decisions to be made (this is called the Quorum) and when the Annual General Meeting will be held each year. The Constitution may also have rules specifying how far in advance of meetings the agendas should be published, and how soon after the meeting the minutes should be made available.

A PTA needs to have a Constitution if it wishes to become a Registered Charity. The benefits of being a registered Charity include the ability of registering for Gift Aid (so that tax can be claimed back on donations) so this is well worthwhile.

If your PTA does not have a Constitution, it is strongly advised that you join PTA-UK. This is a national charity which is set up to support PTAs in the UK. The membership cost is reasonable and is worth every penny as it includes public liability insurance for your PTA, an advice line, assistance in becoming a registered charity if required as well as lots of information and resources including a model Constitution that your PTA could adopt.

Becoming a Registered Charity

Very briefly, if a PTA in England or Wales has an income of £5,000 or more, there is a legal requirement that it should become a Registered Charity. This means registering with the Charity Commission. In Northern Ireland, all PTAs now have to register as a charity whatever their size or income.

Being a registered Charity does mean complying with the requirements of the Charity Commission. However it also brings benefits to the PTA:

-   Means the PTA can receive charitable donations from companies
-   Means the PTA can apply for a range of grants e.g. lottery organisations and charitable trusts
-   Means the PTA can apply for company match funding schemes
-   Means the PTA can benefit from payroll giving schemes
-   Means that the PTA can apply for Gift Aid on donations received
-   Means that the PTA has to have a Constitution (which is a good thing)

Becoming a registered charity is another thing that PTA-UK can offer expert help and advice with, so becoming a member even for this alone is well worthwhile.

Public Liability Insurance

It is very important to ensure that your PTA has public liability insurance. This will cover it for any events held during the year (although you are advised to double check it covers higher risk activities such as pony rides if you are thinking about running them). If you aren't in PTA-UK then you will need to source this from elsewhere.

Lottery and Gaming Licence

If you want to run any events that have an element of lottery or gaming then you will need a Lottery and Gaming Licence from your local Council. These events include but are not limited to raffles, bonus ball draws, 100 club draws and tombolas. As most PTAs will run at least one of these events a year, they should get a Lottery and Gaming Licence. The cost varies between Local Authority but they are not expensive and well worth it in terms of the money that can be raised by doing the activities the licence allows. Contact the Licensing Department at your local Council for more information on cost and how to obtain a licence. You will also need to keep certain records relating to the activities you run such as the amount raised and the amount spent on prizes which will need to be submitted to the Local Authority.

Selling alcohol

If you want to sell alcohol at an event, you will probably need a temporary licence from the Local Authority Licensing Department. You will need to investigate this yourself as requirements can vary but it is mentioned here so that readers know that this needs to be looked into before selling alcohol at an event.

Film Nights

If you want to fundraise by holding a Film Night, you need to be aware that you have to have the correct licences in place or you will risk infringing copyright on the films. Having a film night to fundraise has different licence requirements to having a film for enjoyment. This is something that you need to look into to ensure that you comply with the appropriate requirements depending on the event that you wish to have. There are a wide variety of licences available so this is something you need to research carefully.

6 MEETINGS

The PTA meetings are important as this is where PTA members can discuss and plan current and future fundraising ideas. These can be held as often as you feel is necessary, some PTAs have one every half term and then an additional one if needed, for example if you have a big event coming up. It is very helpful to have a member of staff from the school present at PTA meetings so that they can speak for the school and if needed approve any requests from the PTA for help from the school.

Your Constitution will have some rules about how meetings are run and standard items that should be on every agenda which need to be complied with.

Meeting Dates

Many PTAs plan their meeting dates at the start of the year. This way they are in the diary and the PTA can send out the list of dates to parents once they are booked. Extra meetings to discuss specific fundraising projects can be booked as needed.

As well as the dates, you also need to consider the meeting times. The time of the meeting can make a big difference to the number of people that attend. Remember that you can never please everyone; you might want to consider varying meeting times to give different parents the opportunity to attend. Possible meeting times and their pros and cons are listed in the table:

Meeting Time	Pros	Cons
First thing (school drop off time)	Lots of parents potentially there for drop off time School representative likely to at school	Many parents could be rushing off to work Schools often like to have assemblies first thing so may not be keen for a meeting first thing
Just before pickup time	Suitable time for parents who could come a bit earlier for school pick up time School representative likely to be at school	Parents who work 9-5 could feel excluded as they would not be able to attend
At pick up time	More parents likely to be there as they will be collecting children School representative likely to be at school	Still not suitable for many parents who work Childcare for the children who have just been collected- some PTAs are lucky enough to have a school who will provide a crèche run by another member of staff. If

		your school can't provide this you will need to consider how the children will be entertained if you wish to meet after school and have a productive meeting.
In the evening- at school or another venue such as the pub	More accessible to parents who work 9-5 Can be a good social event for parents	Childcare can be a problem for parents in the evenings especially if single parents or if their partner works in the evenings. Could find the people who can attend daytime evenings struggle with evening meetings. Evening meeting means a long day for school rep, especially if they commute to school from elsewhere so schools aren't always so keen

Making sure people know about the meeting

If people don't know about the meeting then they won't come! This simple rule is important to remember. Ways to tell people about the meeting are listed below:

-Send a flier out to parents with the date and time of the meeting. It's a good idea to make sure this goes out at least a week before to give some notice to parents.

- Social media

Facebook: If you have a PTA Facebook page or group post about the meeting in there. If the School has a Facebook page for parents post the meeting details in there. You could also create a Facebook event and invite all parents in the group / on the page as that will then send reminders to them. Remember to keep the post bumped up so people looking at the page / group at different times will see the post and not forget. If you don't want to create an event, you could tag all parents whilst doing the post as they would then get a notification that way.

Twitter: If you have a PTA Twitter account post details of the meeting there. Twitter moves very quickly so you may find it is a good idea to keep posting about it on there. If you have Hootsuite you can schedule multiple tweets to go out at whichever date and time you wish. You can get a free version of Hootsuite that will allow you to do this. If school has a Twitter account then you could ask them to send tweets about the meeting.

- Word of mouth: Approach other parents at school and ask if they will be coming to the meeting. If people are asked personally, this can encourage them to come.

Maybe not always the first time but persevere, particularly if you have decided to vary the meeting times as different meeting times will suit different people.

- Text: Many schools have a text message service which lets them send a text to all parents. Ask if they can send a text out the day before and then on the morning of the meeting to remind parents.

- Website: If the PTA has a website then meeting dates and papers (agendas and minutes) can be added so that parents know where to look for meeting details- both for future meetings and for minutes of past meetings.

- Noticeboard: If there are parent noticeboards at school, make sure to put fliers up so parents can see them there

- Blackboard: Some schools have a blackboard on the wall in the playground for important messages to parents. If your school has one write that there is a meeting on that day in the morning as another reminder for parents.

Agendas

Your constitution should specify what items are required on your agendas and this needs to be complied with. If you don't have a constitution it is strongly recommended that you get one. A sample agenda with suggested headings is included within this chapter. Of course under each main heading, you would put the actual items to be discussed.

Agendas are vital to successful meeting management because they allow everyone to know what is to be discussed, and should make sure that everything on them is discussed so nothing is forgotten. So as well as being a requirement of PTAs with constitutions, they are also a very useful tool. It is up to individual PTAs and their Committee members to decide on the system that works for them, but usual practice would be for the Secretary to give a closing date for the submission of agenda items before creating the agenda for the next meeting. They would then pass the draft agenda to the Chair for approval prior to publication and circulation.

For maximum effectiveness, agendas need to be circulated ahead of the meeting. Some PTAs circulate them at the meeting, where they are of some use as people at the meeting can see what will be talked about then but they are far more useful if people can see them in advance and think about the different agenda items before the meeting. Seeing the agenda in advance can motivate people to attend if they see that something they are particularly interested in will be discussed. It also makes the PTA more transparent and open which will encourage more participation from parents. Agendas can be put on the website, put up onto social media such as facebook as a document, linked to from the website on Twitter, put onto noticeboards, emailed out to parents or if copying isn't an issue put out to parents in the weekly information bag. How far in advance of the meeting the agenda is circulated is for the PTA to decide, but a week before seems a reasonable timescale as it gives time for parents to read it and for those who are coming to the meeting to prepare for any particular agenda item that they know is coming up for example by researching suppliers for a particular fundraising event that is on the agenda.

Agendas can be put on the website, put up onto social media such as facebook as a document, linked to from the website on Twitter, put onto noticeboards, emailed out to parents or if copying isn't an issue put out to parents in the weekly information bag. How far in advance of the meeting the agenda is circulated is for the PTA to decide, but a week before seems a reasonable timescale as it gives time for parents to read it and for those who are coming to the meeting to prepare for any particular agenda item that they know is coming up for example by researching suppliers for a particular fundraising event that is on the agenda.

X School PTA – Meeting [Insert meeting date]

¡AGENDA

Apologies

Approval of Minutes To approve the minutes of the last meeting held on [insert date]

Chair's Report

Treasurer's Report
1.   Main account: £
     Savings account: £
     TOTAL: £

Items of Expenditure
 To discuss any proposed items of expenditure by the PTA
i). PTA spending (equipment etc)
ii). Requests from School for funding

Event Planning
To discuss any forthcoming events or fundraising activities
i).
ii).

New Fundraising Ideas
i).
ii).

Any other business
i).

Next Meeting
To agree / confirm a date for the next meeting

The Meeting

A few points about the actual meeting:

You need to have a certain number of people present at a meeting for it to be able to make decisions for the PTA. The term for the number of people that you need is called the "Quorum". The specific number required can vary between PTAs but it will be in your Constitution- it may be a number or a proportion of members. If you have enough people at the meeting to make decisions the meeting is Quorate. If there are not enough people at the meeting it is Inquorate. This is a reason to try and ensure good attendance at PTA meetings as it is frustrating if there are decisions that need to be made but can't because of insufficient people at the meeting. If this happens, the meeting can either be cancelled, or go ahead but instead of making decisions that meeting would have to make recommendations which would be ratified (approved) at the next PTA meeting if there were enough people there. For strategic decisions such as long term planning of future events this isn't too inconvenient, but if a decision needs to be made at that meeting in order to book a venue or some other task that has a deadline it can cause difficulties if it can't be decided on that day so it is important to try and ensure that there will be sufficient people at the meeting if there are urgent decisions that have to be made then.

- Hopefully the meeting will run smoothly in terms of what is discussed and not running over time. Keeping meetings running smoothly is a skill that the Chair will find easier as they spend longer in the role. Following the agenda and being mindful of the decisions that need to be made at that meeting helps, and some longer term issues can be deferred if absolutely necessary. Anything that requires a decision to be progressed and that needs to be progressed before the next meeting should be prioritised.

- Some PTAs establish sub-committees with great success. This allows more time to be spent discussing particular issues or events with the sub-committee reporting back to the main PTA for their recommendations to be considered and the decision to be made. Many constitutions stipulate that a Committee member (e.g. Chair, Secretary, Treasurer) needs to be on any sub-committee so it does mean an extra time commitment from whichever of those is on the sub-committee. Sub-committees can can lead to more effective and efficient PTA meetings if they are considering recommendations rather than looking at an issue from scratch so they are worth considering.

- A little thing, but refreshments at the meeting (tea / coffee / biscuits) are nice to have- they a small thing but can help people that have come to the meeting feel appreciated and sharing the biscuits out can be an icebreaker!

Minutes

Every PTA meeting should be minuted. This is so that there is an accurate record of the meeting to refer to in the future as well as at the next meeting. Minutes are also a valuable method of communication with stakeholders (parents, school, the wider community if needed). Sample minutes are included within this chapter.

Minute taking is usually a task that goes with the Secretary role, although if they are unable to attend a particular meeting another committee member could take the minute (as long as they understand that volunteering for this task means actually typing them up afterwards).

Writing the Minutes

The minute taker should take notes throughout the meeting so that they can write up the minutes afterwards. How much they write down varies between individuals- some people can take a near verbatim record of a meeting, others will just take down the important points. As long as the notes are sufficient for the minute taker to produce suitable minutes of the meeting afterwards, how much detail they record is down to their personal preference.

When it comes to writing the minutes for the meeting the following points may be useful to bear in mind:

- Minutes should have a record of who was present at the meeting and who offered apologies for not being able to attend.
- Minutes should follow the same format as the agenda in terms of agenda items becoming minute headings
- Minutes should give an accurate record of the decisions made at the meeting (particularly where decisions involve spending money or tasks that have been assigned to particular people).
- Minute writing is a skill that can take time to get the hang of if you haven't done it before. A word for word account of what was said is not usually needed and would make for lengthy, rambling minutes. Minutes should convey a flavour of what the discussion for any particular item was, with key points of the discussion being recorded without becoming a "he said she said" document that would be difficult to read and make sense of. But they shouldn't be so brief that it is unclear why a particular decision was made. Somewhere in between too brief and too lengthy is what to aim for.

- Every item that resulted in a decision should state clearly what that decision was. It should end with "RESOLVED:" followed by the decision made.

One important point to bear in mind for when the School asks for funding for a particular item:

It is much safer to agree to spend £x on the item and state this in the minutes than to agree to buy a particular item without having the exact quote available. The reason for this is if the PTA agrees to purchase something that the school has requested, and the school buys it before invoicing the PTA (which is how many purchases are made) then there is a risk that the PTA will end up with a much larger bill than it had anticipated. For example if the School requests that the PTA purchases a microphone system and the School representative at the meeting doesn't have an exact quote but says they think they are about £1000 then the PTA could decide "to purchase a Microphone System" but then find that they get a bill for £1500 or more if the School decides on another system, or finds that the system had additional items which had to be purchased with it or the original system that the School Representative had in mind was no longer available. If the minutes state that "The PTA agreed to purchase a School Microphone system" then the PTA will struggle not to have to pay the full amount and an unexpectedly large bill like this can cause stress for PTA members and strain relations with the school.

It is far better for everyone if the minutes are written so that the PTA is only going to have to pay the amount it agreed to spend e.g. *"RESOLVED: That the PTA would spend up to £1000 on the School Microphone system requested by the school. "*. This way everyone knows where they stand, the School will soon get used to this way of working. It is also reasonable to ask that any requests for particular items are presented with at least three quotes for the item so that the PTA can consider how much these items cost and whether they have a preference for any particular item within the quotes. If the School brings quotes for things they are asking for this will save time rather than the request being made at one meeting but then having to ask for quotes to be brought back to the next meeting.

The example above shows how important it is to be careful that the minutes convey exactly what was agreed at the meeting – the difference between the first minute "The PTA agreed to purchase a Microphone system" and the second minute "The PTA agreed to spend up to £1000 on the School Microphone system" is £500 cost to the PTA if the only system available once the School went to order it was the £1500 system. Of course in this scenario, if the second minute had been used the School could come back and update the PTA that actually the sound system was going to be an extra £500 and request further funding but they would have to do this, rather than with the first minute where they could go ahead and purchase it and expect the PTA to fund the full amount.

Circulating the Minutes

Once the minutes have been written, they are draft minutes until they are approved at the next meeting. The first thing to do is for the minute writer to send them to the Chair for their initial approval and permission to circulate them. The Chair can suggest amendments to the minutes prior to their circulation.

Once the minutes are approved by the Chair, they should be circulated. Some PTAs just bring them out at the next meeting but it is far more effective to circulate them soon after the meeting that they are for. This is so that people can see what the PTA is doing- they might want to become involved in some of the future planned activities or see that the PTA is in need of more volunteers and step forward. Having the minutes available gives people a chance to read them before the next meeting rather than skim reading them at the meeting when they have to be approved. Having minutes widely available to any interested parents is really helpful in terms of people feeling that the PTA is open, accountable and accessible rather than being a "closed shop".

If you are going to widely circulate minutes before they have been approved at the next meeting, make sure that it is clear that they are draft minutes. You can easily add a watermarket to the document, just remember to take it off the website copy once they have been approved.

Minutes can be circulated in the following ways:

- Email to parents if you have a list of email addresses (remember to Bcc not Cc)
- Email out to those who attended the meeting (remember the School representative too)
- Placed on the PTA website
- Put on the noticeboard at school if there is one
- Put on the PTA / School Facebook page

It is a good idea to have a folder where all the minutes are stored once they have been approved at the following meeting. This creates an easily found record of what the PTA has done in the past which will be helpful for PTA members in the future. It could either be stored by the Secretary and handed over as new people take over the role, or kept at school. Even if the minutes are also placed on the website, it is always a good idea to have a folder with the hard copies as back up in case anything happened to the information stored on the website.

AGM

The AGM is the Annual General Meeting. As suggested by the name, it is held once a year. It has specific tasks:

- to receive the Chair's Annual Report

- to receive the Treasurer's Annual Report and approve the accounts for the previous year

- to approve the minutes of the previous year's AGM

- to appoint people into their PTA Committee roles (Chair, Secretary, Treasurer plus any others) for the next year.

This is not usually a long meeting as the appointment process is usually over very quickly (unless you have lots of people wanting the same Committee role) but it is important to ensure that each nomination is proposed, seconded and voted upon as part of the appointment process. The proposers and seconders should be included within the minutes for the meeting.

Your PTA's Constitution should specify what agenda items are required in terms of the AGM so this should be your first port of call if you are new to arranging these...... again another reason to have a Constitution if you do not currently have one!

As the AGM is a short meeting, it can be an option to schedule it immediately before a normal meeting of the PTA. Some PTAs prefer to schedule it in the evening and make a social event from it by having it in a pub or restaurant.

X School PTA - Meeting 5th April 2016

MINUTES

Present Jane Smith, Elisabeth Brown, Georgina Hardcastle, Kay Quinn, Catherine Hawkesworth, Mr Morgan.

Apologies Emma Jackson, Rebecca Kendall

Approval of Minutes To minutes of the last meeting held on 9th February 2016 were approved as a correct record.

Chair's Report
Jane reported that the Cake Stall at the recent Village Fayre had been a great success with a large number of donations of cake and other produce from parents and enough volunteers to run the stall easily. She thanked Elisabeth Brown, Georgina Hardcastle, John Bradley, Sue Bell and Carrie Harrison for organising and running the stall so successfully.

Treasurer's Report
1. Main account: £1056.79
   Savings account: £ 779.87
   TOTAL: £1836.66

Elisabeth reported that the bank balances were as above. The recent Cake Stall had, after expenses of £22.86, raised a total of £179.92 which everyone agreed was excellent.

Items of Expenditure
To discuss any proposed items of expenditure by the PTA

i). PTA spending (equipment etc)
Jane proposed purchasing a Popcorn machine from PTA funds. She said that if the PTA owned one, they could then sell popcorn at future events such as the Summer Fair which could be quite profitable so the popcorn machine would pay for itself quickly.

RESOLVED:
i). That the purchase of a popcorn machine be approved in principle; and
ii). That Jane obtain three quotes for Popcorn Machines; and
iii). That this item be brought to the following meeting so that the quotes could be reviewed and a Popcorn Machine be chosen.

<u>ii). Requests from School for funding</u>
Mr Morgan said that the School Staff had recently met and felt that a school microphone system would be beneficial to the school and all pupils. Having the microphone system would enable children to use the microphones at school assemblies and performances and allow the audiences to hear even the youngest children which could sometimes be problematic in a large crowded room without a microphone system to use. Mr Morgan had done some initial research and thought that a suitable system could be bought for approximately £1000.
RESOLVED:
i). That the PTA agree in principle to spend up to £1000 on a school microphone system this school year; and
ii). That Mr Morgan obtain three quotes for suitable microphone systems; and
iii). That this item be brought to the following meeting for consideration of the quotes obtained by Mr Morgan.

Event Planning
To discuss any forthcoming events or fundraising activities
i).Disco
The forthcoming school Disco was discussed. The date for the Disco was confirmed as 21st April 2016 from 5.30p.m. to 7.00p.m.
RESOLVED:
i). The Disco would cost £1.50 per child which would include a drink and a snack; and
ii). Elisabeth would send a flier out in the bag for parents to return with payment prior to the Disco so that numbers attending would be known in advance for planning purposes; and
iii). Georgina would arrange for the purchase of drinks and snacks for the children once the numbers attending were known; and

iv). Kay and Catherine would run a nail painting and facepainting stall for the children at 50p a go. Parents would be informed of this on the flier.

New Fundraising Ideas
i). Kay suggested that the PTA could run a stall at the local Car Boot sale in July. She suggested that parents could be asked to donate unwanted items which volunteers could then sell at the Car Boot *Sale.*
RESOLVED: That this item be brought to the next meeting for further consideration

Any other business
i). There were no other items of business.

Next Meeting
14th May 2016 at 7.00 p.m. at the White Horse Arms.

7 GETTING MORE VOLUNTEERS- IMPROVING ENGAGEMENT

Improving engagement with parents and getting sufficient volunteers is a challenge for most PTAs. It can be frustrating for the people who are involved with the PTA if they feel that most parents are not bothered about the work that the PTA does to benefit their children.

Some tips to improve engagement are below:

- Communication- this is vital! You have to make sure that the PTA tells people about the events it is running, what volunteers or help it needs, how much the events raised and what the PTA has funded. It might feel that most people do not pay attention, but if you stop publicising the work of the PTA then you really won't get any more volunteers so you have to persevere.
- Consider producing a regular PTA newsletter if you don't already. Make it colourful if funds permit to catch peoples' attention and put interesting information in such as what events are coming up, how much money you have raised so far this school year and what you are planning on spending the money on.
- Consultation! Keep asking parents for their views. If you can show that you are taking parents' views into consideration, even if it is just a suggestion for a new fundraising idea that the PTA ends up running, it will encourage people to become involved with the PTA because they will see that the PTA values their views. You do not want to PTA to be perceived as a closed shop, so regular consultation can help prevent this.

- Bribery! Consider running an incentive for all returned consultation documents such as the new parent questionnaire or other consultation exercises that you run. It could be something as simple as having a draw of all the returned questionnaires to win a prize but it may encourage more replies.
- Emphasise how fun PTA events can be, you could do a write up in your newsletter about any event that was particularly enjoyed by everyone who was involved with it.
- Social life- some PTAs have their AGMs as social events with cheese and wine to try and promote the social side of the PTA. How successful this is would depend on your parent population but it is certainly worth considering.
- Good first impressions- try to have a PTA member at the new parent induction evening if your school has one (for the parents of all the children who will be starting in the new school year). If the PTA member can say a few words to inform people that there is a PTA at the school, what it does and what it has bought and is working to buy this can really help engagement with new parents as they have been welcomed on their first visit as parents of children at the school. Consider giving out new parent PTA packs to all the new parents at the induction evening (ideas for what you could put in this are in the last section of this book) and if you happen to have any small PTA branded items such as pencils maybe you could put one of those in the pack too.
- Show the parents how the PTA can benefit them! A good example of this is the second hand Uniform Sale. This benefits the parents as it enables them to buy uniform for their children at a fraction of the price they would pay new. As it saves them money, you are likely to get higher levels of engagement with this PTA activity than others

but it gives you the chance to engage with parents whilst they are buying their uniform. Running the Uniform Sale at the new parent induction evening will reinforce the good impression you have given them of the PTA.

- Communicate in as many different ways as possible! Different people respond best to different types of communication- e.g. some will put most of the bits of paper that arrive in their weekly bulletin bag straight into the bin without reading any of them, but will read everything posted in a Facebook Group. Other parents are avid email readers. If you can use all methods of communication available to you then this should increase the number of people who read the communications and hopefully will increase the amount of engagement you get.

- Talk to people in person! Have a coffee morning every half term. You could do a tea and tissues morning on the first day that the children start school in September- some PTAs find these are really successful in getting new parents who are feeling a bit lost once their little one has started school for the first time in coming for a cup of tea and a chat. They have then met the PTA twice by the time their child has had their first day at school (if you sent a PTA member to the new parent induction) and hopefully will then feel that they would consider helping the PTA.

- Do a new parent questionnaire to identify skills that parents have. Then if you need someone with a specific skill for a particular event you know who to call on. If you speak to or phone the person and say that you remember from their questionnaire that they are good at whatever it is they will be pleased that someone has remembered their questionnaire and hopefully will be happy to at least discuss how they could help the PTA.

- Make sure you keep telling people what the PTA is doing! If people feel they have been involved in an event in some way- even by coming to it and spending money, or donating a prize for the tombola, they will probably be interested to know how the event went and how much it raised. If they know how events did in the end this might raise their interest and encourage them to get more involved in supporting their PTA.
- Acknowledge the help that you do get. It is hard to get volunteers on board so make sure that you keep them there rather than losing them again. If someone has worked on something but then doesn't find out how much the event raised, or is never thanked for the work that they have done then they will not feel valued and are less likely to want to volunteer for the next event.

8 FUNDRAISING- HOW MUCH TO RAISE AND SPENDING THE MONEY!

Basic Fundraising- what is the amount you have raised?

[Amount taken] –[Costs] = Profit

Profit = Amount raised

Seems obvious but in researching this book I found instances of PTAs who did not appreciate this and were quoting the amount taken as the amount raised. Another way of thinking about it is after all your fundraising efforts, and the costs incurred in doing the events- how much money do you have left to spend?

How much money PTAs raise

However much money you raise, it is an achievement to be proud of and it is money that wasn't available before to spend on improving the experience of children at the school. However it is interesting to know how you are doing compared to others, and one way of looking at this is working out how much you are raising per child. There is a huge variation in the amount of money that PTAs raise. I have researched this extensively in writing this book by studying the accounts of over 100 PTAs and found some interesting statistics.

- The average raised by PTAs per child in their last financial year was £29. The amount raised by PTA per child ranged from £5 per child to an astounding £150 per child.
- The total amount raised by all the PTAs I looked at was over £1 million pounds in their last financial year.

- The average raised per PTA was just over £10,000
- The total number of children in the schools / PTAs I looked at was over 35,000 with an average of 352 children per school.
- The smallest school had just over 60 children and the largest school had nearly 2000 children.

Remember the amount that each PTA raises is dependent on many factors- number of volunteers; engagement and support from parents, school and the wider community; the types and amount of fundraising activities done; the affluence of the school's population and wider area (in terms of how much people can afford to spend and also in the amount of sponsorship and donations that can be obtained from local businesses).

If you wish to work out the amount that your PTA has raised last year per child it is an easy calculation to do:

[Total amount raised (net profit)] divided by the [number of children on roll]

E.g: [Total amount raised of £5000] divided by [250 children on roll]

= [£5000] divided by [250]

= £20 raised per child

The figures may not be exact as your school population may vary slightly over the school year, but this is a really useful calculation to do as it means you can see how it has varied over previous years and will let you look at how well you are doing in the future with this measurement. It also means that smaller PTAs who may only raise a couple of thousand pounds per year will not be disheartened if they read about bigger PTAs who raise ten thousand pounds per year as it could well be that by doing this calculation they will see that they are raising more money per child than the larger PTAs.

Spending the Money!

After all the hard work in raising the money, the PTA needs to decide how to spend it!

There are some things that you could consider....

- How to decide what to buy?
    o School wishlist- many PTAs have a system where at the first meeting of the new school year, the school will present its "wishlist" of things that it would like the PTA to consider funding. This can work well as it lets the PTA identify its priorities for the year ahead and allows it to publicise what they are fundraising for which always encourages people to help and spend more as they can see what the PTA is trying to achieve.

In researching this book, I consulted teachers about the things that their school PTAs had funded that they felt made the most difference to the children; and also to them in terms of teaching the children and making a difference to their learning experience. The most popular things with teachers are listed below:

- iPads and accessories (iPad charging station)- overwhelmingly the most popular
- Subsidising school trips- either paying for the transport or donating some of the cost so that the parental contribution asked for by the school was significantly less; or in some cases the PTA and the school split the cost of the trip so that parents weren't asked to

contribute at all which is a real benefit particularly in areas with high levels of deprivation.

- Giving each class teacher a set amount per year e.g. £75-£150 to allow them to purchase items to enhance the childrens learning- whatever they think is needed but examples of things the money could be used for included: cushions for book corner, rewards to encourage good behaviour, stickers, Xmas party presents, specific books.
- Regular donations for new reading books
- Equipment to allow the children to spend more time outside- either Forest School or Outdoor Classroom / Playtrail
- Special activity days e.g. circus or theatre activity days or poet- where companies come to the school to work with the children for the day

o Parent consultation- this can be tricky as you want parents to feel involved to encourage participation and consulting them can help achieve this, but you also want to be buying things that are actually needed by school. If a parent suggests something that sounds fantastic and it is bought by the PTA, it would be a real shame if it was never used as that would be a waste of money that could be spent on something else. Ways round this might be the PTA sending out a survey with suggestions of things that the school has suggested and that the PTA is happy to fund and saying that the most popular one is what is bought; or parents could be asked to make suggestions and the most popular ones taken to a PTA meeting for discussion with the school (to make sure that it is something that is useful and that would benefit the children by being used) and consideration by the PTA to choose which one to fundraise for.

o Children consultation- asking the children what they think would improve their time at school can be worth doing; it is always fascinating to see what they suggest, and often the things that they suggest are not very expensive so they are not asking for a huge amount of money. Think about how to do the consultation- many schools have a School Council with a child from each year group which can be utilised as a source of ideas. Other ways to consult children might be for the PTA to either ask classes for suggestions (teacher help here is useful) or do a questionnaire to get ideas followed by a vote to find the most popular suggestions to take to the PTA meeting for consideration (and consultation with the school to ensure they would be suitable and used). If the cost of what the children is asking for is low, it might be worth considering allocating a small amount of money to each class to allow the items to be purchased. It is nice to go back to basics and find out what the children would like rather than what the PTA or school think they need from time to time, and really satisfying to see their faces when they get the items. It can inject new enthusiasm into the PTA members and the children telling their parents about the new items they have got from the PTA can only help in terms of awareness and goodwill towards the PTA.

School budget vs PTA funding

This is a subject that different PTAs and schools will have different views on. The relationship between the school and the PTA will be influential here as the better the relationship between the two, the more likely it may be that the PTA is sympathetic to the requests from the school. Essentially the PTA needs to decide how it feels about what the school requests and what it will consider funding- this sounds easy but it can lead to debate about whether some things should be funded from the school budget (e.g. tables, chairs, dining furniture) or whether the PTA should pay for them. Many PTAs take the view that if the school says it needs it then they will support that and fund it, others do not. Ultimately it is the PTA who decides what they spend their money on, not the school so it is worth considering where your PTA stands on this should it ever come up. As school budgets get tighter and financial pressures on schools increase, this is something that will come up more often.

Decision making

This may be obvious, but it is worth a reminder. PTA funding decisions should go through the meetings. If your PTA has a constitution it should say this. You want to be able to show how decisions were made, and what the decisions were, and that they were made by the PTA. This is done by having the decisions considered and made at PTA meetings which are minuted to show this information. This keeps the PTA open and transparent and accountable to everyone involved with it.

You do not want to end up in a situation where a member of school staff is coming to individual PTA members and asking them for funding for particular things- this potentially could put them in a difficult position and could also leave them personally liable for the decision they made if they said yes but then at the next PTA meeting the official decision was no and money had already been committed by the school purchasing something because the individual PTA member agreed. Making sure that all decisions go through the PTA meetings protects everyone involved, and everyone knows where they stand. It might take a little while to get used to if this isn't how your PTA has worked before, but as long as everyone who needs to know is told (PTA members and the school) they will soon get used to it and should see the reasons why. This also prevents the awkward situation where you might have a PTA committee member who is also being employed by the school being asked if the PTA will fund something by a member of the school staff who if senior could be their boss- the PTA member could find it hard to say no and be placed under unfair stress in this situation.

Of course you will want to avoid the situation at the other end of the scale where a PTA member wants to buy something of a low value for the PTA such as if they have come across a bargain on Christmas wrapping paper for a few pounds. Good communication and perhaps having policies in place that say PTA committee members could spend up to £x amount without prior approval, or that they can buy it but the expenditure when they reclaim the money has to be approved prior to payment at the next meeting will help everyone know where they stand to ensure proper decision making processes are followed but retaining some flexibility to allow PTA members to purchase things they know will be needed if they happen to come across them at a bargain price.

Another option

Some PTAs agree to donate the money that they raise directly to the school. The Headteacher then arranges for the money to be spent and ensures that parents are informed that the PTA has raised the money and what it has been spent on. This does seem contrary to the traditional way of the PTA deciding what to spend the money on, but it can make sense for some PTAs. It means that if the school needs an item, the Headteacher is able to purchase it with the money and means that they do not have to wait for PTA approval at the next meeting. It also means that there is no risk of disagreements within the PTA of what to spend the money on, or for PTA members to feel under pressure to decide one way or the other on particular requests- either from the school or other parents or PTA members.

A compelling argument for this way of working is that the parents and PTA trust the Headteacher to ensure their children are safe and well educated at school, so they should trust them to make best use of the money for the benefit of the school and the children. In these days of ever increasing budget cuts and deficits, it could be said that the PTA will be needed to fund whatever benefits the school and not necessarily the "extras" as in years gone by. Of course this will only work for some schools and very much depends on the circumstances of individual schools whether this system is preferable but it is an option. If the PTA was considering moving to this way of working, they would need to make the decision officially at a PTA meeting before doing it. A half way house option could be where the PTA retains a certain amount of money to spend on things like allocating money to classes, Xmas books and smaller things, but resolves to give £x to the School at the start of the school year for the Headteacher to spend on what they felt was needed for the School.

9 MUST DO FUNDRAISERS

This section highlights some of the activities that I would classify as "must do". They are "must do" because of the benefit they can bring (financial or otherwise) for less effort than some of the other fundraising activities that PTAs can do. Whilst many of them will take time to set up initially, they are then either relatively low maintenance, or the returns that they can yield make the efforts in running them worthwhile.

All of the activities detailed in this section are explained more fully in the A-Z of fundraising ideas section.

- **100 Club**: This is a must do because after the initial setting up phase, once the numbers are sold (which happens at the beginning) then the PTA has received all the money from the event. Then all they need to do is run the regular draws through the school year and pay the winners. Once this has been set up for the first time, subsequent years take less effort because the systems are already in place and many people will keep their numbers throughout their time with the school so you are unlikely to have to sell all of the numbers again.
- **BagstoSchool**: This is literally money for old rope (or clothes). You can expend additional effort by having PTA members collecting BagstoSchool donations throughout the year, but the basic model just requires parents to be asked to bring any unwanted old clothes to school on two specified dates per year. Then the company collects the unwanted clothes and the PTA gets paid! The payment is made according to the weight of the clothes collected so there is an incentive to collect more, but

any amount raised is worthwhile particularly as it is such an easy fundraiser to do.

- **Big Event**: I would suggest having one Big Event a year. This gives an opportunity for the whole school community to come together for it (or just the parents if you choose to have a Ball) but these can become much anticipated events. They are hard work, but can raise a lot of money and if you are only doing one a year then PTAs tend to find the work worthwhile. Some PTAs do more than one Big Event a year and that works for them, but if not seriously consider doing at least one.

- **Christmas Raffle**: These seem to raise more than raffles held at other times. Some PTAs find their Christmas Raffle raises almost as much as their Christmas Fair! Some work is required in terms of sourcing attractive prizes that will encourage people to buy tickets, and selling the tickets but the returns are worth the work required.

- **Easyfundraising**: I am a big Easyfundraising fan. It is literally free money. If you can get your parents into the habit of using Easyfundraising whenever they do online shopping, they will earn their PTA commission on whatever they spend doing their normal purchases. So it doesn't cost them any money (and can actually save them money as there are often special deals available through Easyfundraising) and can raise a significant amount of money for the PTA if you get enough people to sign up and use it.

- **Grants**: Not enough PTAs try to apply for grants for projects they are doing. The process appears daunting, and is time consuming to get right. But the chance to get hundreds or thousands of pounds for a day or two of doing grant applications properly makes it worthwhile if you have someone willing to do it- if you are successful the rate of return in terms of money raised for the time spent getting it is very high.

- **Matchfunding**: More free money! If the PTA can find out if any of the parents at the school work for a company that does match funding, and the PTA meets the criteria of that company, all they need to do is to get that parent to help at an event and then potentially double the amount of money the event has raised as match funding means the company will match what the event raised by itself. Find out what the exact criteria are for any match funding scheme your parents might be on- if a parent is going to help out at your Christmas Fair and the company will match what the stall that parent helped on raises, make sure the parent is helping out on the stall that is likely to raise the most money to maximise the amount of money gained.

- **Sponsorship**: There are various ways to make money from sponsorship which are detailed in the A-Z. Again, there is some work in setting it up, but if you can persuade a company to pay £200 for their logo to be on the PTA newsletters for a year that is well worth the effort.

- **Supermarket loyalty vouchers**: These are the vouchers that supermarkets give out from time to time to customers. The amount of vouchers given out increases with the amount that each customer spends. The more vouchers you collect, the more free equipment you can exchange them for through the supermarket's scheme. Again, this is essentially free equipment- the PTA just has to try and encourage people to collect them and donate them to the PTA.

- **Uniform Sales**: This is more effort as the PTA has to get people to donate old uniform and then wash it and sell it at events. But I have included it as it is cost free- the PTA isn't having to pay for what it is selling so the money it makes is nearly pure profit. But the more valuable benefit is that it is going to appeal to any parent who wants or needs to save money on the costs of buying school uniform, and this gives the PTA the chance to engage with more parents as they use the Uniform Sales, and makes many more parents aware of the existence of the PTA and then they may become interested in becoming involved with it.

10 A-Z OF FUNDRAISING IDEAS

This chapter has two sets of Fundraising Ideas. The first is an A-Z of ideas that can be done as standalone fundraisers. The second is an A-Z of smaller fundraising ideas that could be incorporated into a larger fundraising event such as a Christmas Fair.

Each idea is explained, however some may be covered in more detail elsewhere in the book in which case this will be stated in the explanation for that idea.

100 Club

This is an easy way of raising money. Parents "buy" a number for a year. All the numbers are put into a draw and the people who own the numbers that have been drawn win a cash prize. Once the numbers have been sold and the payments banked, this is a low maintenance fundraising method. All that has to happen then is for the draw to be done and cheques paid to the winners.

For example, if you had 100 numbers and sold them at £5 each you would get £500.

If you had a draw each term where two numbers could win a prize of £25 to the winner and £10 to the runner up that would be a total of £105 paid out in prize money. If you did an additional draw at Christmas where the winner got £35 and the runner up got £15, that would be a total of £150 in prize money, leaving a profit of £350 for the year.

If you have a larger school, you could make it a 200 (or more) club. If doing this though, it could be wise to consider either an increase in the value of the prizes slightly, having more prizes to win each draw or having more draws to ensure parents feel they still have a chance of winning and that it is worthwhile joining. You could make numbers more widely available such as to other members of the childrens' families, teaching staff and school governors if you didn't manage to sell them all to parents.

If you wish to run a 100 Club, you would need to have a Lottery and Gaming Licence from the Council.

Art Exhibition

A more unusual fundraising method, but one that can work well. Possibly more suitable for Secondary Schools than Primary Schools but worth considering. The art at the exhibition comes from the art work the children do at school (some of the art that Secondary School children produce is amazingly high quality and desirable). All the art is available for sale to people who come to the exhibition and this is where most of the money is raised. These events can be surprisingly popular and become an anticipated annual event locally.

Tips:

- Think about getting an unusual venue for the art exhibition- somewhere a bit different that you can display large amounts of art. Just to add more of a sense of occasion, but if not the usual village hall or even school would work too.
- You want to invite a large amount of people to the exhibition (the more people that come, the more sales you are likely to make). This is definitely an event to open to the wider community as well as just parents.
- See if you can invite your local Mayor to come and open the exhibition – they will be keen to support their local school and it will add to the atmosphere of the event. Mayors are incredibly busy however so you will need to invite him / her as far ahead as possible or they will

probably already be committed on that date. If you have the Mayor coming, you can also state this when you are doing publicity material and it might increase your chance of getting a write up in the local paper ahead of the event.

- Have a real publicity drive for the event- information out to parents as usual, but also post widely on social media (not just the parent only facebook page). Create an event on facebook that people can invite their friends to and ask that they invite people they know who might want to come. Approach local galleries and invite the owners, put posters up where you think they will be seen by people who might be interested in attending an art exhibition, get the event listed in the Local Event section of the local paper (and try and get them to do an article about it too).

- You could charge a small entrance fee to people coming to the event, but the bulk of the profit is in the art sales. You need to decide if charging an entrance fee would put people off, but if you think you can get away with it, this will help offset the PTA's costs in putting on the event.

- Offer everyone coming to the exhibition a drink on arrival- either a soft drink or wine. Again, adding to the sense of occasion and as an icebreaker to make people relax into the event and hopefully buy more art! If people have drinks they will need to stay a certain amount of time to have their drink and hopefully look at the art while they are there. Obviously if you are selling alcohol you will need to make sure you comply with the licensing requirements where you are.

- If you can run a bar at the event this will boost the amount of money that you raise significantly. It also means that people will stay longer if they decide to buy another drink which increases the potential of them seeing a piece of art that they want to buy.

- You will need to have a system in place for the artwork on sale- for each piece you will need to know who it is by, how much it is, whether it is sold or still for sale and if it is sold who has bought it and whether they have paid. If you have any parents who run art galleries or are artists (most artists will have been involved in an exhibition at some point) you should ask them for assistance with this. If not to run the event, at least for some guidance on how to set up your system for this.

- Make sure all artwork on display is clearly numbered and priced so that buyers know how much they will be spending if they buy the piece, and to tell the person in charge of sales which painting they want to buy. Many exhibitions have a simple system of putting a small red sticker on a painting in an exhibition once it is sold so that this is clear (so you don't risk selling it twice!!). Don't let people take the pictures home immediately, you want your exhibition to stay intact for the evening or it will lose its impact to later arrivals if artwork is disappearing from display! This means you will need to record contact details for every buyer, whether they have paid on the night or will pay on collection and have arrangements in place for how and when buyers will get their artwork. It is probably sensible to have one person in charge of recording the sales made on the night and getting the additional information, with assistants as required.

- Have all the volunteers at the event dressed up smartly, again to add a sense of occasion to the event.

Bag Packing (at supermarket)

Supermarket bag packing is a good way to raise money as it is (hopefully) getting donations from the wider public rather than from parents. You have to contact the supermarkets to apply for permission to bagpack. Many supermarkets allow charities and good causes regularly and will allocate you a "slot". Depending on how popular bagpacking at the supermarket is with local good causes you may find that you are allocated a date some months away.

Tips:

- If you are limited in volunteers to do the bagpacking, it is better to have all your volunteers together bagpacking for say one hour than have less volunteers for a longer time. This is because if every till has a volunteer, people won't be able to avoid the tills that have bag packers there. Obviously customers can choose whether they wish to have their bag packed or to donate, but it also looks better to have a volunteer at each till even if it is for a shorter time period.
- Have the children wearing their school uniforms for greater appeal to the public.
- Have one adult to each till as well as a child. In practice, it is the adult helpers who will do most of the bag packing although the children will want to help but adults are quicker and breakages are less likely! The children, especially if little ones, may get tired fairly quickly so they need an adult there to help them.
- Make sure you have a bucket for every volunteer for customers to put their donations into. Have a large notice on each on to show what the good cause is such as "St Michael's PTA" to encourage donations.

BagstoSchool / textile recycling

This is a great way to fundraise as it is easy to do and can generate a reasonable sum depending on the size of your school. The PTA asks parents to donate old clothes and textiles which they no longer want on a particular date. The company comes and collects the donated clothes and the PTA is paid for the weight of the collection. At the time of writing, 40p per kilo is the amount paid. This doesn't sound like a huge amount, but old clothes are heavy and if everyone brings a binbag it does mount up. A small school can raise £200-£300 in one collection if parents donate well, a large school could obviously raise more.

Tips:

- Make sure you send the special bags out to parents in good time so that they have time to do the clearout. The recycling company will send these out about a month in advance.
- Make sure parents know exactly what can or can't be donated. For example pairs of old shoes are fine but towels are not. If it doesn't state this on the bag, consider sending a flier out to parents with the collection bag.
- Remind parents about the collection- on facebook if you use this, also if the school uses text messaging to parents, ask them to send a text to all parents the day before so parents don't forget to take their donation to school!
- If you have storage space, consider asking parents to donate throughout the year. This can yield more donations in the form of clothes that parents have cleared out but are unwilling or unable to keep until the next BagstoSchool collection date. Send a bin bag with a flier on explaining that parents can fill this at their convenience and either return immediately or once it is full works well, particularly if sent out just after Christmas and the Summer holidays as many people have clearouts then. Doing this doesn't seem to reduce the amount collected on the normal BagstoSchool days so is an effective way of increasing the amount you collect. Be warned though- you really do need significant storage space to do this!

Ball / Black Tie event

Some PTAs raise a significant proportion of their money in a year by holding a Ball / Black Tie event. It is a large event to organise, so will be time consuming but the potential amount raised makes this worth considering.

Tips:

- Consider what sort of event you want to run. Do you want to combine it with a Promise Auction? (many PTAs do, but obviously this adds an extra element of work to do in the form of securing donations / administering the auction).
- Where will you have it? For a big Ball / fancy event you could either go with your village hall (many PTAs do this with great success and deck it all out for the evening so it doesn't seem like just the village hall) or consider a hotel or other venue. Consider how much you could sell tickets for and that may help you decide if you want to have the event in your village hall (more work but means you could sell tickets more cheaply as much less expensive to put on) or in a local hotel (more expensive but potentially much easier for the PTA to run, especially if you decide to get the hotel to do the catering too).
- Who will you invite? Parents only? The wider community? Again decide what works for your PTA- parents only is good if you think you will have enough demand from parents to buy all the tickets. But wider community can work too- some PTA Balls are well supported by and looked forward to by the local community as an annual social event, particularly for smaller village schools. Opening it up to the wider community means that you are giving other people the chance to support the school, and giving you the opportunity to raise money from outside the usual parent population of the school.
- How will you cater for the event? For a Ball / Black Tie event, people are going to expect food and drinks. Can the PTA cater or would it be easier to get caterers in? Or could the hotel do a special deal because it is for a charity. If you know what your costs are going to be you can calculate the price of the tickets so that you make a profit after covering your costs (venue, food, a drink with the meal, other costs such as venue decoration, entertainment). You can then boost funds raised with a raffle or Auction.
- Getting caterers in might seem expensive, but it is worth

considering in terms of how much easier the event will be to manage if you just have to pay to get the food provided as this means not having to organise food production for large numbers of people and volunteers to make and serve it. If you do decide to cater the event yourself, consider running a buffet system so you have servers at the buffet but aren't having to serve people at tables individually. You would need to carefully work out what food you were going to provide, and how much of it you needed for the number of people coming and find volunteers to make / serve it. Potentially there is more profit to be made this way but more work involved. A buffet system can make for more of a community feel to an event however.

- Sell the tickets well in advance and take payment well in advance so that you are getting money in to cover the costs of putting on the event.
- If you are having a bar you will need to make sure you comply with licensing requirements.
- What entertainment will you be providing? Have you any bands / singers that would do your event for little or no cost or would you be better paying for one? Factor this cost into your ticket price too.

Bingo Night

This can be a fun, social, way of fundraising. The event could be held for parents only (consider the implications of parents having to find childcare and the effect this could have on attendance) or for parents and children to attend. It could be held either at the school or in another local venue, perhaps a village hall (cheap to hire).

Tips:

- You will need to get the bingo cards and pens in advance. You could either make the cards or they can be bought quite cheaply (easier). See if school will let having to buy those.

- You will need to have a way of generating the numbers. You could number a load of pingpong balls and put them in a truckle tub / bucket and have someone draw them out. Or you could use cloakroom tickets and a bucket.
- Consider how you will raise money- how much do you need to charge per bingo card? What sort of prizes will you be offering eg money / other prizes? If other prizes could you get businesses to donate or use something you have left over for another event? You want the prizes to be worth entering for but not cost any more to provide than they have to.
- Raise extra money by selling simple refreshments such as tea / coffee / juice / crisps. These can easily be bought in bulk at most supermarkets cheaply enough to be sold on at a reasonable cost to participants but still allowing some profit to be made.
- Check whether you need to have a Local Authority Gambling Licence in order to run a Bingo event

Bonus Ball

This is where you sell individual numbers that match those used by the National Lottery. If you can sell all the numbers for say 50p each a week that would raise £29.50 per week. The person with the winning number could win £15 meaning it would raise £14.50 per week. Doesn't sound that much but there are 40 weeks of school term a year so 40 x £14.50 is £580 per year which is a worthwhile amount. If you can't sell all the numbers, as long as you can sell most you could just roll the prize over each week that a "vacant" number comes up.

Tips:

- Sell the numbers annually so everyone pays £20 at the

start of the year (if you're selling at 50p a week x 40 school weeks) and it will be a fairly easy way to raise the money.

- There are companies that will run the bonus ball for you. These may be worth looking at, but they take a proportion of the subscriptions that you collect so that you would make less profit, and if you can't easily sell all the numbers it may not be a viable option.
- You would need a Lottery and Gaming licence from the Local Authority to run a Bonus Ball scheme.

Book event

It is lovely to run an event involving books as pupils enjoy it, and it promotes a love of books and reading. There are lots of different ways to involve books in an event. Some suggestions are below:

- Sponsored Read / Readathon

Ask the children to do a sponsored read of a book of their choice or the school's. Send sponsorship forms home with children so that they can ask friends and family to sponsor them either for the event or by the amount they have read in the event. Then school can run a session with PTA support to allow the children to do their reading to earn their sponsorship money.

- Book swap

Ask all the children to bring an unwanted book or two into school and the money (whatever is deemed appropriate for your school- 50p might be a reasonable sum). If you can borrow the school hall, have the books laid out there in category such as early reader, adventure, animal etc and then the children can come in by Class / Year Group and choose a new book each. Any left over books afterwards could be sold after school for 25p each or kept to make a PTA book stall at the next large event such as summer fair.

This is a great event for children as they get to choose themselves a new book. Consider any children that haven't been able to bring a book or the money and perhaps let them choose a book anyway- this event is probably going to be more about letting the children choose a new book to foster a love of reading than making lots of money so it might be better to let them choose a book and benefit from the event than exclude them from it.

- World Book Day

Children love World Book Day! Often the school will be running events linked in to World Book day, but if not the PTA could consider running an event, or in conjunction with the school. Children could dress up and make a donation towards the PTA and perhaps there could be a competition for the best costume in each year group who could win a prize.

- Book Fair

There are various book companies that will come and run a book sales event at the school. Many schools are savvy to this and will already be organising one of these a year, but if not they are worth investigation by the PTA. The school hosts a book fair using books supplied by one of these companies, with fliers going out in advance to notify parents. Parents can either come in at pick up time to purchase a book with their child, or the children can be sent into school with money. The children get to choose a new book which again encourages reading, and the book company gives the School / PTA "commission" on the books bought at the book fair. The "commission" isn't cash but is in the form of a credit that the school can use to buy books for school. These events are popular and can enable the school to get a large number of new books for the school without having to spend any money, so they can be very useful.

Bounce event

Children love bouncing! This probably works best with a bouncy castle but trampolines might be a possibility. If you can tie this in with an event where you will have a bouncy castle at the school anyway that is even better as it means you won't be paying extra to hire one (unless of course your PTA owns one or you have a friendly parent who can supply one). Send sponsorship forms home with the children to ask friends or family for sponsorship either per bounce or for the event. Then have the children do their bouncing in groups- decide how many bounces they need to do to get their sponsorship form stamped perhaps ten or twenty. For peace of mind and also time reasons it is probably more sensible to have the children only need to do say ten or twenty bounces than to continue indefinitely for their safety in case they over exert themselves. The children love these events and they are a reasonably easy way to raise money.

Buy a Brick

This is a great fundraiser if you are raising money to build something- whether an extension, a whole new building or something else. You can decide how much to charge per brick and write out to parents. You could say that everyone who donates a certain amount will get their name on a plaque, and then have a higher sum where donations at this amount get the person's name engraved on an actual brick to be used in the build. You would need to ensure that the design of the build was suitable for this so that the named bricks could be used in a way that the names on the bricks would be visible once the build was complete. There are specialist suppliers who will sell bricks engraved with the names of your choice- at £8 per brick if you could sell them for £30-£35 each then that would be a good fundraiser. For projects of this nature, it is worthwhile approaching local businesses to see if they would be willing to sponsor a brick (or more), making sure that you emphasise that their named brick would be on display in the finished build so it would be a great advertising opportunity.

Cake Stalls

The traditional PTA fundraiser! But for a good reason, people like them and they can raise enough money to make running them worthwhile. Cake Stalls can be run as standalone events, particularly if you can take them outside the school environment and into somewhere else such as your local high street (some towns allow charities to have fundraising cake stalls- the Parish Clerk of the Parish Council covering the high street you are interested in will be able to tell you), or car boot sales or a larger village fayre. Having a cake stall somewhere that you will have different people to the usual parents as customers is good as they will have the novelty of your cake stall, and any event that allows money to be raised without asking the school parents for money is a good thing as often PTAs are worried that they are asking the parents at the school for money too often and are very aware of this.

Tips:

- To encourage donations, some PTAs like to send out a paper plate in the bulletin bag the week before with a rhyme or verse on it asking for parents to fill and return the plates
- Some PTAs like to send out information about a cake stall well in advance with a list of suggested cake types and asks that people specify what they will be donating so that they know what they will get and what they need to ask people to make in order to have a varied selection

on the day
- Cake stalls don't just have to sell cakes! Some PTAs, particularly in rural areas, sell fresh eggs donated by chicken keeping families on their stalls- these are always popular. Homemade jams and chutneys if people are willing to donate them are also popular.
- If you have willing volunteers, there is nothing wrong with getting them to bake cakes / scones / whatever they can bake that will sell well and allowing them to reclaim the cost of the ingredients from the PTA. As long as you get receipts for everything so that the Treasurer can arrange for reimbursement to the volunteer (or the PTA could just provide them with the ingredients) this can be a good way of boosting the amount of stock you have to sell on the day to raise as much money as possible.
- The Showstopper Cake!

If you are lucky, you will have a parent who is really good at baking cakes! Not just the normal scones or cupcakes (although these are good too) but something really impressive. If you did a skills audit then this might have identified a suitable person, or perhaps you could send out a flier saying the PTA is looking for advanced cake bakers, or you might know from word of mouth. If you get really lucky you might have such a parent who is looking to start up a cake baking business or has one already and who is keen to build their portfolio and increase their exposure as a business.

If you can identify a suitable person, see if they can be persuaded to make an amazing cake for the next cake stall event if the PTA will provide / pay for all the materials needed. If they want to put business cards on the stall next to the cake that would be a reasonable arrangement if it persuades them to make the cake. On the day, instead of just selling the Showstopper Cake, raffle it off! Use a book of cloakroom tickets as raffle tickets and if you can charge £1 a ticket and make sure you put peoples' mobile numbers on the ticket stubs then you should raise a lot more money than just selling it, be able to contact the winner easily for them to collect it and if your cake baker can get exposure from having one of their cakes on your cake stall as a raffle prize then everyone is happy. Getting £60-£80 in raffle ticket sales for a showstopper cake is not an unreasonable expectation- more for a larger school or event so it is most definitely worth doing.

- Arrange in advance with the school that should there be any leftover stock from the cake stall that it can be sold after school on the next school day (eg if the cake stall was at the weekend, the leftover stock can be sold after school on the Monday). Reduce the price of everything for sale to half price and you should be able to sell most of it. Confirm with school in the morning that you will be selling cakes half price at pick up time and ask them to send a text out to parents to let them know. Also post on the PTA/ School Facebook and Twitter pages so that as many parents as possible know to bring their money!

Car Boot Sales

There are two ways to raise money using Car Boot Sales:

Having a PTA stall at a Car Boot Sale:

- Ask parents for donations of unwanted items such as bricabrac and books / DVDs / CDs for the PTA to sell at their stall at the Car Boot Sale. If you can arrange for items to be donated on the Friday before the Car Boot Sale (assuming that it is on at the weekend) will mean donations will only have to be stored for a minimal amount of time.
- Have the PTA stall staffed by volunteers- the PTA will need to arrange who these will be in advance so that they can get organised in advance for the Car Boot Sale e.g. get table, make sure they can get the donations from school etc in time to attend the Car Boot Sale

- At the Car Boot Sale, once you get the feeling that it is quietening down don't be afraid to reduce prices on the stall- you want to minimise the amount of stock that you take away with you and as it was all donated any money you get for it is money raised.
- Any left over clothes / shoes / bags can be kept for the next BagstoSchool collection if storage is available. Any other left over stock can be donated to charity unless the PTA can use it for anything else such as future tombola prizes but clearly the amount saved for future events depends on the amount that can be stored.

PTA running a Car Boot Sale:

- Some PTAs run their own Car Boot Sales with great success.
- Decide where to have the Car Boot Sale- can you use the school as a venue? Or would it be better to use an established venue? Some car boot sales that are run regularly at the same venue are actually run by charities with the land owner allocating a date to different charities to allow them the chance to run a Car Boot Sale in aid of their charity. If there is an arrangement like this at a Car Boot Sale in your local area, you will need to see if they have any dates available, and be prepared to accept a date well in advance. Be aware of school holidays- whilst running a Car Boot Sale on a Bank Holiday weekend can be more lucrative in terms of people attending, it can be harder to find volunteers willing to help with the event as they may be away with their families.

Carols

Children singing Carols is lovely!

The PTA can either choose to help out at a Carol event on a "breakeven" basis or look at using Carol singing as a fundraising event.

- If the school does a Carol singing event, the PTA could support it by selling refreshments for the people who attend the event. These could be the childrens' parents, or members of the wider community. Some schools do a special Carol singing event for members of the wider community in order to maintain and improve the school's relationship with its community.
- If the PTA is running a Christmas Fair, the children Carol singing could be incorporated into it. This can work well for a number of reasons:
  - o Children who have to do something at a school event will boost attendance at the event by parents / family members / friends as the children need to be brought to it which hopefully means whilst they are there they will participate in it, even if they just buy a cup of tea or go to a couple of the stalls it is all extra potential fundraising income.
  - o If the Christmas Fair is inviting members of the public, this allows the school to invite members of the wider community to it to hear the Carol singing which means they don't have to do a special Carol assembly within school time (some will think this is a positive, others will prefer to still have the special service). This is also a good opportunity for families to invite grandparents / aunts etc to see the children singing as it can be harder for them to attend school assemblies due to lack of space in assembly halls or not being able to attend during the school day (Christmas Fairs are often held either after school or at the weekends).
  - o If the PTA is selling CDs of the children Carol singing, it can have these available at the Christmas Fair where potentially more people may wish to purchase it having heard the children singing.

Catalogue Sales - Yellow Moon etc

This is where the PTA sends out catalogues to parents in the weekly information bag. The parents are asked to return orders and payments to the PTA by a specified date. The PTA then submits the orders to the company, and distributes them to parents once they have arrived. The PTA earns a certain amount of commission from this. These schemes have been lucrative in the past, but the increased popularity of internet shopping seems to have made some catalogues less popular with parents than before. That said, many parents do enjoy looking through a catalogue so if you have a volunteer who is willing to administer sending out the catalogues, collecting and submitting the orders to the company and then distributing the orders to parents once they have arrived then it is definitely worth considering.

Tips:

- Research the companies that offer this facility to PTAs and decide which one(s) you would like to do
- Once you have chosen which one(s) you want to do, consider the best time of year to send them out to parents- the Yellow Moon and Webb Ivory ones could do well sent out so that parents can purchase items for Christmas from them so in the Autumn term. However if you wanted to do a Seed catalogue, people choose seeds over winter so maybe just after Christmas (the company will be able to advise you).
- Find out from the companies how long they take to return the orders once submitted and factor this in when planning when to send the catalogues out, and how long to give parents to return orders as you don't want everything to arrive when the school is on holiday as this would mean parents would be waiting longer for their items to arrive.
- Some companies who do these catalogue schemes now also have an internet shopping website. These tend to be

where the PTA registers with them to get a special code for people to enter into the website whilst they are shopping. The PTA then gets commission on orders where the customer has entered their referral code. The PTA would send out details to parents on a flier with the code and website address asking them to look at the site and to enter the code if they decide to order anything. This is easier than sorting out catalogues / orders etc yourself but may not yield the same return. You could send out the catalogues with the code so that if parents see something that they like from the catalogue but prefer to order online then hopefully they will use the code.

- Check with each company how they work the payment- some like the PTA to collect all the payments to send with the orders to the company, others prefer the PTA to get parents to pay them and then the PTA send the company the money minus the commission amount. As each company doing this type of scheme does it slightly differently, it is important to research carefully to ensure you are happy with the method your preferred company uses.

CD of children singing (Christmas Carols)

Selling a CD of the children singing can be a popular fundraiser as people like the chance to purchase something with their child in it, and it is a nice memento for when the children are older as well as being something that the family can enjoy now. There are companies that will come out and record the children singing and then create a CD for the school to sell. The PTA / School can choose the cover that is used in the CD case. The PTA takes the orders for the CD and pays the company their cost for the CD and then sells the CD on to parents for the cost to purchase the CD plus their mark up to make a profit. Some companies do not charge for the recording session.

Tips:

- Any singing can be used for the CD, however Christmas Carols are a popular choice because it means they can be bought by parents as Christmas presents for other family members which can boost your sales. It also means that you could sell CDs at your Christmas Fair if you have the children singing carols there so potentially gaining more sales there.
- You will need school to help with the logistics of getting the recordings of the children singing the carols for the CD as this is done in school time. If school is doing a Carol service or assembly then hopefully this could be combined with rehearsals that the children are doing for this event.
- A nice way to get the children involved is to run a competition for all the children to design a front cover for the CD- the winner gets a prize and their picture is used for the cover. You could also run a competition for them to choose a name for the "band"- again the winner gets their name used and a prize. You could give a small item such as a pencil to all the children who enter the competition. This is a great way to build awareness of the CD before it is made and you start sending out order forms to families.

Children's Art- calendars / teatowels etc

There are numerous companies that will take childrens' pictures and turn them into calendars, tea towels, plates, mugs, key rings, bags and various other items. The basic way that it works is that the PTA supplies the children's art work to the company who will put it onto whatever item is ordered at a certain cost, and then the PTA sells the finished items to parents at a price that includes a mark up to allow the PTA to make a profit on each item.

Tips:

-Think about the logistics of the different items that are available. Do you need to have one image of artwork per child or can you come up with one image that can be used for all of the items? Obviously it is easier if you just have one image, but you may find that sales would be higher if all the children's images were used as it is harder for parents to resist if they know it is their child's picture on the item.

- How will you get the images? If one per child then you will get better participation if they can be drawn in school time rather than asking children to do them at home and bring them in.

- If you are using one image, you could run a competition to encourage entries to choose the winning image from.

- Could you use multiple images from all the children (e.g. handprints) on one item so that it appeals to all the parents but is much easier logistically as all the orders will be for one thing rather than having to match each parent's order to the correct image

- Ensure you have planned the timescales from the children doing the pictures, the PTA submitting the orders to the purchased items arriving for distribution in relation to the term times of school as you may not want them to arrive in the holidays

Christmas Cards

As for Children's Art above, there are also many companies who will take children's pictures and turn them into Christmas Cards. They tend to be a popular seller as it is hard to resist buying cards with a picture that your child has drawn! Take the price that the PTA is charged per pack of cards and add a mark up to determine the price that you will sell them for so that you make a profit on them.

Tips:

- Using an image for each child so that parents can buy cards with their own child's pictures will boost orders but will be more effort for the PTA to collate and sort orders.

- This works best if school will allow the children to do their pictures in school time- this means that all the children have done a picture and they are more easily collected in than if the children are asked to do them at home and bring them in

- As for art work above, plan the timescales carefully- there can be a leadtime of a few weeks between submitting the orders and them being delivered and you will want to ensure that they are sent out to parents in good time for them to be able to use them as Christmas cards.

Christmas Raffle

The Christmas Raffle can be a seriously big fundraiser! Raffles tend to do well anyway, but the Christmas ones seem to raise more, perhaps because there are more opportunities to sell the tickets and perhaps because people in a Christmassy mood are more willing to purchase tickets. In some schools, the Christmas Raffle can be 15% of the amount raised by the PTA in the year.

Tips:

- For a big raffle, you could get special tickets printed. They should give the name of the promoter (check with your Local Authority who this should be but many schools put the name of the Headteacher and details of some of the prizes on offer). They should be numbered.

- If this is the big raffle of the year, consider making the price more than you would charge normally for raffle tickets- say £1 a ticket. The better the prizes you are offering, the more you can charge but you don't want to make it so expensive that people don't buy the tickets.

- Consider sending out numbered tickets in the weekly bag and asking families to sell them to friends and family (and returning any unsold). This is something PTAs shouldn't do too often because parents soon get fed up with getting sent things to sell and often just buy the tickets themselves to save having to sell them but if you are sending out 5-10 tickets a family this gets expensive for them. On the plus side, if you are going to do this it should yield a reasonable number of sales.

- If you are going to send numbered tickets out for parents to sell, the following suggestions can make it an easier process:

    o Keep a list of which number tickets went to each family and tick them off as either the ticket stubs and money or unsold tickets are returned to school

    o Give a deadline of at least a week before the day of the raffle draw as a deadline for when all ticket stubs / money / unsold tickets have to be returned. This gives time to chase up for any that haven't been returned by then (if you have kept the list of tickets and families you will be able to see who hasn't sent them back)

- Start planning your raffle weeks or months in advance. This will let you write out to local businesses to ask for donations for your raffle. You could also ask parents if they have anything new and suitable for a raffle that they could donate. You will need to know what your main big prizes are before you get the tickets printed so that you can say what some of the prizes are on the tickets.

- See if school is willing to donate a prize or two. A Christmas hamper is always popular and can be done at a low cost if the staff are willing to donate an item each to be made up into a hamper. You could have a School Staff hamper and a Governors hamper if you are lucky! Running a non uniform day to get the children to bring in items suitable for making into hampers is also an option although if you are having a Christmas Fair you might want to get them to bring in tombola prizes instead but you could always take a few items out to make a hamper as well. Once you have the items, you just need a basket or box to put them in with some cellophane and ribbon that can be bought cheaply from a florist or online and it will look really impressive. If you make the hamper (s) up in good time, you can take them to events where you will be selling tickets to encourage people to buy them.

  o For selling the tickets you could do this in different ways:
  o Send out to families (as mentioned above)
  o See if local shops and businesses would sell them (make sure you get all stubs / money / unsold tickets back at least a week before as above)
  o Tie in with the Christmas school events- if you are having a Christmas Fair you could take the best prize (e.g. an impressive hamper) and have

people selling tickets at the Fair

o Sell at the school's Christmas performances- many schools have at least 2 performances to allow all parents to attend, or split the performances by class / year groups so if you can get volunteers to sell tickets at all of these that is a great way to sell to grandparents and other family members. Get the Headteacher to mention that the tickets are being sold at the performance and if you can have the impressive hamper or whatever your headline prizes are at the performance that will also encourage people to buy tickets.

- Have the draw at the last Christmas event of the year, whether that is the school's Christmas performance or the Christmas Fair- this gives you the maximum number of events to sell tickets.
- Keep an eye on the number of tickets you have left, if you find you have sold most of them by putting them out to families in the bag, you might want to order more tickets. This is another reason to have the deadline for them coming back at least a week before the raffle.
- Remember to record the prizes and number of tickets sold in case you need to submit the form to the Local Authority as a condition of your Lottery and Gaming Licence which you would need to have to run a Christmas Raffle.
- When selling the tickets remember to make sure that the contact details (name and telephone number) of the person buying the tickets are recorded on each of the stubs.
- Hopefully you will have sold a large number of tickets before the day of the draw. Start folding them and putting them into the box or whatever the day before as this can be time consuming- that way you just have to add the ones sold on the last day before the big draw! It isn't fun to be rushing to do this before the draw.

Christmas Present Grotto / Room

This is a very similar idea to the Mothers / Fathers Day shops. The PTA buys in lots of presents at a certain price and then allows the children to choose gifts for their family members at a price which allows the PTA to make a profit.

Tips:

- Remember to factor in the cost of the gift wrap when calculating the price you are going to charge per child / gift.
- Christmas Present Room is different to Mothers / Fathers Day shops as rather than just buying one gift, the children are likely to want to get a few gifts for various family members. You will need to think about how to price the event accordingly- could you do three gifts for £5 for example?
- As for Mothers Day / Fathers Day, if you can have a sample item of each type of gift on display but have the rest of the stock prewrapped this will save a lot of time on the day of the event.
- You will want to have a wider range of gifts available than for your Mothers / Fathers Day shops as you will need to provide gifts that children would choose for Mums, Dads, brothers and sisters. This can be done but it does mean the event will be on a larger scale than the Mothers / Fathers Day shops.
- Because this event is larger, it may be worthwhile seeing if there is somewhere you could set up your Christmas Present room over a day or two to get all the children through and allow them to choose their gifts from the larger selection.
- If you can get a room / corner of a hall for your event, you can make it all Christmassy with the use of wrapping paper, tinsel, a fake Christmas tree if you can borrow one and any other Christmassy props you can get hold of that still allow you to have room for all the gifts and will withstand all the children coming to choose their gifts.

- Children do love getting to choose gifts for their loved ones, so this is a popular event with the potential to raise some money, so it is worth considering.

Clothes swapping / swishing

This is a fun way to fundraise and good as you can consider doing it at a different venue to school and inviting members of the wider community. Basically everyone has to bring some items of unwanted clothing that is still in good condition and pay an entry fee. People get a token for every item of clothing they are donating. They then "spend" the tokens on any other clothing that they like- one token for each item of clothing they want.

Tips:

- Consider running this at a village hall as these are cheap, accessible and have plenty of space
- See if you can get some clothes donated beforehand so that you have some "stock" already there when the first people arrive
- You will need some clothes rails to hang stock on, as well as tables to put other items on. See if you can borrow the clothes rails.
- You could also allow people to donate good condition shoes or bags and have a special section for those
- Consider how you will organise the stock- having a clothes rail for each size would be a logical way to do it, making sure that the sizes are clearly shown so everyone knows which rails they need to look at
- Make more money by selling refreshments (tea / coffee / cakes) at the event. This also potentially gives time for volunteers to take the donations from people and add them to the clothes rails while the first arrivals have their cups of tea before they start looking at clothes.
- Have a plan for what to do with the left over stock after the event. It will need to be removed from the venue immediately after the event- have binbags to put it in. If you can keep it for the next BagstoSchool collection that

is an excellent way of boosting your BagstoSchool total.

- If you have someone who likes eBay who is willing to go through the leftover stock to identify and remove items that are worth selling on eBay that is another way to boost income from the event.

Coffee mornings - at school or external venue

Coffee mornings are a nice way to raise extra funds and are nice social events. Sometimes the PTA might provide teas and coffees for free (such as if they are running a coffee morning for new parents) but they are also a good way to fundraise.

Coffee mornings can be done at the school or in another venue. If you research, you may find local venues that have a weekly "slot" for good causes to come and do coffee mornings there. These are fantastic because they often have a core group of "regulars" who will go each week so you will have some customers plus the ones you can get from advertising at school and further afield. If you can find a venue like this, they are well worth looking into but bear in mind that they are very popular with the organisations that run the coffee mornings so you may be allocated a date quite some time away, or have to go onto a waiting list for any future spaces that may come up.

The other sort of venue that you may be able to find depending on your location is a one that allows good causes to sell refreshments but for a whole day or even a weekend. These types of places are often in tourist areas so have a passing trade of walkers and tourists who will pop in for refreshments. As before, these book up well in advance if you can get in at all, but they are worth looking at because the PTA can raise a lot of money. Consider carefully the logistics involved with running something like this for a whole day or weekend in terms of staffing it and having enough supplies for the whole time.

The other option if you don't want to have a coffee morning at school is to hire a local venue such as the village hall and have it there. Village halls are good venues as they are usually a reasonable cost to hire. This is a less attractive option in terms of not having an existing base of "regulars" or "passing trade" but will be much easier to book sooner than the other sorts of venue if there are any near to you.

Tips:

-Research carefully to find all the venues locally that you could get a slot at if you want to do an outside venue. Find out the date you would be allocated from all of them so that this can be considered when the PTA decides if it wants to do a coffee morning at a venue like this. Also take into account any "regulars" or passing trade in the form of tourists / walkers when deciding which venue to go with.

- Make an action plan of what supplies are needed, who is supplying them, what volunteer support is needed and a rota as well as how the event will be advertised and who by. If you can plan this early on it will make it easier to fill the volunteer spaces and for advertising to be done.

- See if you can add another fundraising element to the event- a tombola is always popular and a good fundraiser but check with the venue first to make sure they don't mind you doing this or whatever other idea you have.

- If you go with a venue that is in a nice area with walkers etc, consider if inviting the children for a sponsored walk or similar would work as a nice activity / excursion as well as hopefully getting more school people to come to the venue to buy refreshments.

- Think about the possible weather when you are planning what refreshments to serve. If it is going to be in winter and cold then soup is a popular choice and also a great fundraiser as delicious soup can be made easily and cheaply. If it is going to be in summer, consider if there is freezer space available and if so whether you want to sell ice lollies / icecream in case it is a hot day. Ice lollies and icecream are also great fundraisers as supermarket own brands can be bought cheaply enough to add a decent markup without making them too expensive to sell.

- Internet shopping is fantastically helpful for ordering supplies for largescale events where you are selling drinks and food. You order it and it arrives so you don't have to buy it all at the shop. Ordering the day before is sensible just in case something is out of stock so that you have time to go and get that item, but generally internet shopping is a great timesaver. It is easier than having to make a trip to the cash and carry and buying in bulk can bring the prices down to the cash and carry prices or less in some cases.

Cooking Demonstration event

Cooking has become very popular in recent years with all the television programmes about many different types of cooking. This means that a cooking demonstration event is likely to be well received- it is something a bit different and something that can be done in the evening to make it more of a social event for parents or in the daytime for the whole family so can be adapted by the PTA to suit their circumstances / parent group etc to encourage maximum participation.

Tips:

- Does anyone know any chefs that could help? Famous ones would be great but failing that any contacts anyone has with local chefs could be useful to try and find one or more to come and do cookery demonstrations at the event. If nobody knows any chefs, try approaching local restaurants to see if any of their chefs would be willing and able to come and do some cookery demonstration work. If any PTA members are regulars at local restaurants so are known to be good customers they might be the right people to approach them. As well as helping the PTA, this could be a real opportunity for the chef / restaurant to showcase their food and have a large number of potential new customers tasting the food they cook. As it could benefit the chef as well as the PTA, it is well worth asking until you find someone.
- Plan the menu with the chef who is doing the demonstration well in advance. You need to know what will be cooked so that you can make reference to the dishes in the promotional material for the event, as well as planning what supplies you will need to purchase for use at the event.
- Sell the tickets in advance so that you know how many people will be coming. If you are struggling to sell enough then you will know you have to do more to sell them rather than find not enough people turn up on the day.
- See if the chef will offer some sort of discount at their restaurant for everyone that has tickets to the event. If you can say when advertising that all tickets will get a 10% discount on their food at x restaurant, that will add value to the cost of the tickets and encourage sales. You could make a real point of people having the opportunity to see the chef cooking his dishes and then getting a discount to go and eat at the restaurant. The restaurant is likely to be agreeable to this as it is better publicity for them and has the potential to gain a large number of new customers.

- Decide how many people you can accommodate for the event- you want to sell enough tickets to make it a worthwhile fundraiser and event, but not so many that people are so crowded that they can't see the cooking demonstration. You will need to work out the costs of the event (venue hire if not at school, ingredients, publicity material, advertising etc) so that you can calculate how much to sell the tickets for in order to generate a decent profit on the event.
- Think of ways to boost what the event raises by adding extra fundraising methods such as:
  o Sell refreshments: tea / coffee / soft drinks etc – again if bought from supermarket it is possible to sell these at a reasonable cost to the customers but still make a profit
  o Could you run a tombola or run a raffle with donated prizes (perhaps saved from a previous prize collection exercise such as a non uniform day) or buy some in
  o Could you have any related stalls at the event? If you have a local shop that does cookware maybe they might be interested in coming with some of their products. You could charge them a small fee (say £10) for the stall plus something from their stock to raffle off. Having a cookware stall will help add to the overall theme of the event.
  o Consider producing a recipe book to tie in with the event. Make it one that can be sold afterwards too but if you could get the chef to provide recipes for what he is making at the event these could be put into the book to encourage people at the event to buy it. The recipes can mention the chef and the restaurant so that is encouragement for the chef to help with this as it is another way of publicising their restaurant.
  o Consider the logistics of the demo itself- what equipment will the chef need, where will he be

situated to ensure that the guests can all see the demo, will the chef need to actually cook and if so can someone supply a portable hob / gas ring for him to use (as he will need to be in the hall for the people to see rather than in the kitchen).

o For publicity you could contact your local paper to see if the cookery demonstration can be listed in their local events section, or even have a small write up to increase publicity and encourage ticket sales.

Craft Fair

Craft Fairs can be really fun events for volunteers and participants alike. You can invite people who make their own crafts to have stalls at the event, and then provide other stalls with craft activities for the children. You could then have a cake stall to earn some extra money, and perhaps a tombola. If the PTA can sell other refreshments such as tea / coffee / bacon rolls that will make the event more fun, keep people there longer because they will be able to buy food there rather than having to leave if they get hungry and will increase the amount of money the event raises.

Alternatively, you could decide to have a Crafting Event just for the children as a "break even" event where you put on different crafting activities for the children and charge a small amount for them to come to help with the costs in running the event. These can be really fun and enjoyed by children, adults and the PTA volunteers who run the stalls.

Tips:

- Decide on the sort of event you want to run: Craft Fair to raise money and therefore open to the public; or Craft Event for the children to do as a break even event. Knowing which sort of event you are running will help you decide on the venue- fundraising event could be school or a village hall; break even craft event for the children is more likely to be in the school hall if available.

-Craft Fair as Fundraising Event:

- o Work out how many stalls you can fit into your venue. Remember to book spaces for the stalls the PTA wants to run to boost fundraising (e.g. tombola and cake stall). Then you can book the other stalls out to people who want to sell at the event.

- o You don't want to make the fee too expensive for your stall holders, but you should charge a fee to let people have a stall at your event. £10-£15 a stall will contribute towards your costs in running the event. You could ask all stall holders to donate something to use as a prize- either individually or you could quickly pack up all the stall holder donations into a nice hamper to raffle off on the day. If you can get 10 stall holders at £10 each plus a prize donation that will be £100 towards the cost of your event plus whatever you can earn selling tickets for the raffle.

- o Have a form for all stall holders to fill in and return to you with payment for their stall. Take payment in advance so that they know that they have secured their stall and you know (notwithstanding emergencies / illness) that they will be coming. If people have paid for a stall in advance they are more likely to come so that you aren't let down on the day with lots of empty stalls. Make sure your form has contact information for each person and a description of what each stall is selling so that you can try to ensure some variety in the types of stall and prevent duplication as if you ended up with lots of stalls selling very similar products it wouldn't be as interesting to the people who come, and the stall holders probably wouldn't be very happy as they would be competing against each other for sales. A variety of stalls makes for a more interesting event for the people that come to the event.

o   There are lots of people who have crafting as a hobby or home business so you should find it relatively easy to fill the stalls. You could let parents and school staff know first so that they get the chance of a stall if they want one. Any leftover stalls are usually easily filled with a few posts on social media- posting in local selling / mums pages on Facebook will usually find people who want to have stalls at a Craft Fair.

o   If the PTA can run a stall with crafting activities for the children, this is always popular and again means people tend to stay at the event longer (so spend more money) as their children won't get bored as quickly.

o   Make sure that you can get the venue from a bit earlier than when the Craft Fair is due to start so that there is time for everyone to get set up. Tell all your stall holders they have to be there and set up before the event starts so that it is all ready when people start to arrive.

-Children's Craft Event:

o   Decide when you are going to have it- a Saturday morning is nice but then you are probably asking school staff to come in on a weekend which is a very big ask indeed. If Saturday morning isn't an option, consider after school.

o   If the event is just for children to do crafting, you will probably be asking parents to drop their children off rather than staying with them. On a Saturday morning, you might find this is quite popular as it gives parents who aren't helping the PTA a chance to go off and do some shopping or whatever once they have dropped the children off. As you will have the children for a couple of hours or so, consider including a drink and a snack in the cost of the event so that everyone is fed halfway through. Factor in the cost of this into your ticket price- although you might not be running it as a fundraiser, if you can make the event break even by not spending too much more than you are taking then this will save your PTA funds for other things.

- o Plan the activities you are going to do with the children in advance. This will let you source supplies as cheaply as possible, and see if you can do activities using materials that you could ask the children to bring into school to minimise the cost. Pinterest has a wealth of crafting ideas for inspiration!
- o When it comes to doing the event, if any of the materials you are going to use need cutting into shapes it is advisable to do this in advance as much as possible. Once the children are there doing the activities, the volunteers will find that they are occupied helping them and will struggle to cut out more materials at the same time. It is far easier to have everything prepared in advance.

Crowd Funding

This is a relatively new phenomenon in the world of fundraising, and has taken off with the advent on the internet. Basically you can set up your project on a crowd funding website giving details of the project and your target and hope that people will donate an amount towards the target. Whilst this might not be such an obvious way of fundraising for day to day PTA spending, it is worth considering if you have a particular large project that you are fundraising for such as a new building or major outside play area project. If your project is either unusual or you can demonstrate really well how it will make a real difference this will increase your chances of raising money with a crowdfunding scheme.

Tips:

- Research the different types of crowdfunding schemes available before you sign up as there are different sorts that work different ways.
    - o All or Nothing (fixed funding): These schemes are set up so that if the target isn't reached within the specified target time, the people who volunteered to donate money are not charged so you wouldn't get any money paid to you, even if some people said they would donate to the project.
    - o Keep what you raise (flexi funding): These schemes do allow the project to receive the money pledged by donors, even if you don't hit the target within the specified time.
- Be aware that many crowd funding companies do charge a fee to the project that they raise money for by way of a deduction from the money that is paid out. This percentage varies by company, scheme and whether the project reached it's target or not. Make sure you completely understand what the fees are before you sign up to any crowdfunding scheme. You can factor the cost of the funding into your target so for example if the fee for the scheme you choose is 5% of donations and you need £10,000 you could make the target £10,500 so that after the £500 fee (5% of £10,000) is taken off, you would still have your £10,000 to spend on the project.
- Crowdfunding encourages that donors are able to get "rewards" for donating to schemes. The "rewards" given vary by the amount pledged by the donor. Suggestions for possible rewards are below but you could decide on whatever works well for your PTA / school and that you

think might entice people to back your project:

- o £10 donation- certificate to commemorate your donation to the project and photograph of the finished project emailed to you
- o £25 donation- certificate to commemorate your donation, thank you letter from the children and photograph of the finished project
- o £50 donation- certificate to commemorate your donation, personalised thank you letter written by one of the children and a photograph of the finished project
- o £75 donation- certificate to commemorate your donation, personalised thank you letter written by one of the children, your name engraved on a plaque of appreciation to be displayed in the building and a photograph of the finished project
- o £150 donation- certificate to commemorate your donation, personalised thank you letter written by one of the children, your name engraved on a plaque of appreciation to be displayed in the building and a 12x8 canvas print of the finished project
- o £250 donation- certificate to commemorate your donation, personalised thank you letter written by one of the children, your name engraved on a plaque of appreciation to be displayed in the building, a 12x8 canvas print of the finished project and invitation to the opening ceremony of new building as an honoured guest
- o £1000 donation- certificate to commemorate your donation, personalised thank you letter written by one of the children, your name engraved on a plaque of appreciation to be displayed in the building, a 12x8 canvas print of the finished project, invitation to opening ceremony of new building as an honoured guest and the new building named after you

-The above are just suggestions, but demonstrate how the "reward" values increase as the donation amount is increased. If you can think of "money can't buy" rewards, these may tempt people to pledge a bit more. You might as well think of a reward value for a really large donation- you may not get one of that value but you never know! You will spend a bit of money fulfilling all these rewards, but as long as the cost of each reward is only a small proportion of each donation amount then it is well worth the effort as effectively you will make a healthy profit on each donation that you get.

-The key to successful crowd funding is getting the scheme known about. This is where you will be asking absolutely everyone that you know- parents / teachers / friends / family / workmates to share the link on social media to maximise exposure and therefore increase your chance of getting donations.

Dog Show

Dog shows can be surprisingly popular! It's not every PTA that runs a dog show as a fundraiser, but there are some that do quite successfully. You can choose to have a companion dog show which means you would have classes like Waggiest Tail, Best Rescue, Fancy Dress, Best Trick, Best child handler etc. rather than the sort of dog showing you would think of if you've ever watched Crufts on television.

You need a good venue (outside is better than inside) with plenty of space for dogs, showing rings, stalls, people and parking. If you are interested in running a dog show, you can contact the Kennel Club who will be able to provide you with information about what classes you could have, how the Kennel Club licensing process works and the requirements to get one; and how to obtain insurance for the event.

Tips:

- You need to make sure that you are properly insured to have a dog show. If you already have public liability insurance you need to check whether running a dog show would be covered, if not you will either have to extend your cover if they will permit it, or purchase specific public liability insurance for the dog show from another provider.
- If, after researching information from the Kennel Club, you have decided you want to do a dog show it offers some good opportunities for working with other local charitable organisations and getting sponsorship for the event.
  - See if there is a local dog rescue who would like to come and have a stall at the event. Don't charge them for the stall, you want them to come along and publicise the event to their supporters as they will want to encourage them to come to help them raise money (they often do a tombola type stall which is fine as this doesn't stop the PTA also having a tombola if they want to). Hopefully the rescue supporters will come along to enjoy the dog show and spend money at the other PTA stalls. You could have a Best Rescue class in the show as an extra encouragement to rescue dog owners to come along.
  - See if a local dog food company will sponsor the show in some way- they could provide the prizes for Best In Show and each class winner. They might sponsor the rosettes too if you are lucky.
  - You could just do prize cards for your winners, but it is much nicer to get a nice rosette if you win. There are lots of companies that do rosettes by mail order and they are not particularly expensive. You get standard rosettes for the winners in each class (you could do rosettes for 1st, 2nd, 3rd and then prize

cards for 4ᵗʰ and 5ᵗʰ if you wanted to save a bit of money), and then a bigger rosette for Reserve Best in Show and the biggest rosette of all goes to Best In Show. If you can do a little prize for all the participants in the child handling class that is a nice touch. Have all the rosettes for each class in separate envelopes so they are ready for each class without having to find one of each place before each class.

- o You will need to find a judge! See if any of your parents do dog showing and are in any local showing clubs that might be willing to come along.
- o For organising your show- you will need to produce a Schedule which is a list of all the classes that you are running. It is easiest for a Companion Dog Show to take entries on the day. Which means you need someone with a desk, a cashbox, a gazebo (in case it rains) and a folder to record the entries for each class. You also need forms and pencils for people to fill in to enter their dogs when they get to the show, and that is when they pay to enter each class. Make sure the schedule says clearly what time judging starts so people know when they need to be there for. You will need a Steward to help the judge and to shout out what class is next.
- o As well as running the dog show which hopefully will raise a bit of money or at least break even, you can then have extra fundraisers there such as a tombola, raffle, selling tea / coffee / soup and a cake stall. These will all increase the amount that you make. If you advertise the dog show well enough you should hopefully get a worthwhile number of people coming along.

Duck Derby

A Duck Derby is a charity event where hundreds of numbered plastic ducks are released into a river. Every duck's number is sold (like a raffle ticket) and the winning duck(s) win the ticket owner a prize which is usually money. They are usually run as events with some stalls by larger charities inviting other charities to take part with them. All the charities involved are allocated tickets which they need to sell and the ticket money is split between the charities selling the tickets and the main charity who is organising the event. All the charities are usually invited to run one or more stalls at the event so it is a nice way to do a fundraising stall or two but with people that aren't the usual school parents.

Tips:

- If you can find a local Duck Derby event, you will need to contact the organisers to see if they have a vacancy for a new charity. If they don't, you can ask to be put on a waiting list in case a vacancy comes up.
- If you are able to join a Duck Derby event, you will be allocated tickets to sell. You can put some out to parents to sell to friends and family or to return unsold ones to you by a specified date. If you do this, make sure you keep a list so that you know which ticket numbers went to each family in case you need to chase up outstanding tickets that haven't come back. This is very important as if you can't return unsold tickets, you will be liable for the organising charity's share of the ticket money for the missing ones.
- Parents need to return the stubs for the sold tickets, the money and any unsold tickets so that you can either sell them elsewhere or return to the organisers. Once you have all your tickets / stubs / money returned, you will need to return the tickets and stubs to the organisers

along with their share of the money from the sold tickets.

- If you are going to have a stall at the Duck Derby, consider what sort you want to do. Make sure the organiser doesn't have any restrictions on this but if there aren't any, cake stalls and tombolas tend to do well. If you have room for a breakeven activity for children who come (nail painting / face painting etc) this is enjoyed and is a fun part of the day.
- If you do decide to participate in a Duck Derby, do remember that due to the nature of the event it will be held near a river, and consider what you need to put in place to ensure the safety of any children attending the event with you.

Easyfundarising / online shopping schemes

Easyfundraising is fantastic way to raise money. Essentially it works by getting people to choose an online retailer through those listed on their website (www.easyfundraising.org.uk) and then directs them to the retailer's website- then if the person buys something with that retailer it will generate commission which comes back to the PTA. Once set up, it pretty much runs itself although the more you do in reminding people to use it and getting more people to register with it the better it will do. It helps all sorts of good causes, not just PTAs but thousands of PTAs use it. Once you have got supporters signed up to the scheme and using it regularly you should find that it raises enough to generate a payment into the PTA bank account every three months- how much that is depends on the number of supporters registered and how much shopping they do. The easyfundraising website has a table of all the PTAs registered with it and how much they have raised- those in the top 10 of fundraisers have raised between £4500 and £10000 through the scheme which shows how much can be raised and how worthwhile it is to use as a fundraising method.

To begin, you register your PTA with easyfundraising as a good cause. This is quick to do, and then you should be activated as a good cause within 48 hours (they have to verify that all new applications are genuine good causes). Once your PTA is live on their website as a good cause, you can encourage people to register with the site and choose your PTA as the good cause they support.

When someone is registered with the site (which again is very straightforward) they just need to do their normal online shopping that they would do anyway (there are thousands of online retailers on the site including really commonly used ones such as eBay, Amazon, Marks and Spencers, John Lewis, Argos, Thomas Cook, Next, Sky). The only thing they need to do is to go to the easyfundraising website first to be linked to the retailer they are going to so that a commission is generated. There is a Donation Reminder that can be downloaded so that it reminds people if they are shopping at a retailer that is affiliated with easyfundraising and gives them the option to activate the donation. There is now also an app that people can download onto their phones or tablets so that they can access the retailer they want that way. Donations vary between retailers , but can range between 0.5% to 15% of what you spend.

Common questions about easyfundraising from parents:

   -Does it cost me anything?
No, you do your online shopping exactly as you would have before at the retailer's website. The only difference is that you go to the site via the easyfundraising website so that the commission is earned. PTAs aren't asking people to spend more, just to do the shopping they would have done anyway but through the easyfundraising site so that their spend can earn commission for the PTA.

-Can people see what I've spent / bought?
No. When you register with easyfundraising, you can choose to appear as anonymous. If you don't select this and get into the top ten of supporters for your PTA, it will just show your first name and initial e.g. Helen J and the amount that you have raised in total. The PTA's easyfundraising admin will be able to see what purchases have been made by the cause's supporters and how much each one has earned the PTA, but not who made the purchase.

-Is it worth registering- will I raise enough to make it worthwhile?
Absolutely it is! As the saying goes, every little helps. The more people that register the more you will raise, even if people are only earning a few pence on any transactions they make it soon adds up. If people only use it when they are shopping with Amazon and eBay that will generate enough donations to make it worthwhile, often as people get into the habit of using it they will go to the easyfundraising website whenever they are going to buy something online to find the website they need, and chances are it will be on there as there are nearly 3,000 retailers registered with the scheme. Retailers on the easyfundraising scheme often offer special deals to customers purchasing that way- so the supporter can save money by shopping that way as well as raising money for the PTA.

Some retailers offer a sizeable donation- e.g. Sky gives a donation of between £5 all the way up to £54 depending on what is bought and whether it is for a new or existing customer. Insurance (car / home / pet) purchased through the site, or if you book your holiday (hotel / flights / package holiday) through the website can also generate large donations. Easyfundraising will email supporters whenever a new donation is logged from one of their purchases so that they are updated on what they have raised for the PTA. They can also log into their account to view their donation history. Small regular donations can also add up- for example at the time of writing, Sainsburys will donate 50p for any supermarket delivery order- if you use them for your regular supermarket delivery those 50ps will soon add up.

Tips for the PTA

-Someone will need to register with the site initially so that they can register the PTA as a good cause. They will be the easyfundraising admin so can see more on the site than people who are registered as supporters, but won't be able to see what individual supporters are buying / spending- just the transactions.

- There are lots of resources on the easyfundraising website to help good causes encourage people to register and use the scheme such as fliers, posters, premade social media posts and information on current deals.

- If you have any questions about easyfundraising- either as you are setting it up or at any point once you are registered, you can contact them for assistance. They are very good at answering queries so it is always helpful to remember you can contact them if needed.

- There is now an easyfundraising facebook group for the easyfundraising admins of the different causes who use it. This is a useful resource and worth joining if your easyfundraising admin is on facebook.

- Once you have set up your PTA as a good cause with easyfundraising and it is showing as a good cause on the website you can start getting people to register! You might decide that before you launch it you have the core PTA members signed up and using it so that you can show people that it is already raising money, or you can just launch it immediately. Some ways to publicise and encourage this are below:

- Social media! Facebook / twitter are both great as you can post a link to the PTA's page on the easyfundraising website for people to sign up to support.

- The PTA website (or schools if they will let you)- you can put the link on with a bit of information to tell people they can help raise money for school / PTA if they register

- Fliers: Put a flier out to all parents in the weekly bag. You can download flier templates from the easyfundraising website so they are easy to produce.

- Posters: Again, you can download poster templates from the easyfundraising website- if the PTA has noticeboards at school put them up there and see if you could put one up in the staffroom for the school staff too.

-You can get hand out cards printed quite cheaply if you shop around- you could put the PTA cause name, the easyfundraising website address (www.easyfundraising.org.uk) and a reminder to use it whenever they are shopping online to help fundraise. These are really useful as you can take them with you whenever the PTA has a stall somewhere that the general public are so they can be given out there, or put into the new parent information packs, or given out to new parents at their induction evening before the summer holidays (so potentially they could be raising funds before their children have even started at the school!).

- See if school will let a PTA member do an easyfundaising demo at a parent assembly. Letting people see for themselves how easy the site is to use is really effective in getting them to sign up and use it. Most schools have a big screen in their assembly hall that is linked to a laptop which the school uses, if this can be used for your demo it works very well. When I did this after about a year after I had set easyfundraising up for our school I saw a real increase afterwards in the number of supporters we had. If you want to do this, bear the following in mind:

- The school needs reliable internet. You do not want it to crash halfway through your demo! If you think this might be an issue, you could consider having a powerpoint demonstration with screenshots as a back up in case the internet does go down during your demo. There are sample presentations available to download on the easyfundraising website.

- You will need to do a test run a few days before in terms of making sure that the easyfundraising website can be used from the school computer- some school IT systems are very strict so school might need to phone their IT provider to arrange for their computer to be able to use the easyfundraising website for your demo. Obviously you need to test this before the day of the demo!

- Have a flier / hand out card to give to everyone who is at the assembly to take away with them so that they can use the information to register with the site whilst it is fresh in their mind.

- While doing your demo and showing people around the easyfundraising website make sure to show people the Top 10 of PTA Fundraisers (at the bottom of your cause page) so that people can see how much money other PTAs have raised with the scheme.

- If it is the easyfundraising admin who is doing the demo (this makes sense as they will know most about it) they can also show the screens that the easyfundraising admin for the cause can see- this will help allay any concerns parents might have about whether the PTA will be able to see what individual supporters have raised, and also will demonstrate how even little donations will soon add up (helps if you have a few donations already there if you want to do this).

- Coffee mornings- if the PTA is having any coffee mornings or similar events, if you can have someone there with a laptop to demonstrate easyfundraising to people there this is effective because it gives the opportunity to talk to people individually and if they like help them register with the scheme there and then.

- Publicity! The easyfundraising website also has templates for press releases for good causes to use. If you can get your local paper to write an article about how the PTA has signed up and would like as many people as possible to sign up to help raise funds to support their local school this can be an excellent way to get more supporters.

Once you have registered and got some supporters registered and shopping you should see that the amount raised will keep increasing with time. It is a good idea to keep reminding people to use it- particularly coming up to Christmas when many people shop online more as they are buying presents, when people are booking holidays and any other time you can think of. Easyfundraising will send regular emails to the PTA admin to suggest reminders that can be sent out to parents- again using social media / fliers etc. Another effective way of encouraging use of the scheme is to have a Special Offers thread on the school or PTA's facebook pages- details of any sales or special offers available through easyfundraising can be posted there. Also remember that your parent population will change each year as the new intake joins the school so you need to make sure that the parents of the new children are encouraged to join too.

Easyfundraising also offers other ways to raise money:

- Easysearch

This is a search engine. People would use it like any other search engine e.g. google but for every search that they do it raises 0.5p. Again definitely a case of every little helps but if you can get people to use the easysearch search engine every time they look for something on the internet it soon adds up. See if people will encourage colleagues to use it for all their work related searches too. The more people that use it the better and it is paid together with the donations raised from the online shopping so is no more admin work from that point of view. You need to go to the easysearch part of the easyfundraising website to get the specific link for your cause, and can then start publicising it with social media and putting the link on the PTA / school website. You could also create hand out cards to give out to people to put by their computers to remind them (and also encourage them to bookmark the page as a favourite or homepage so that it is easy to find when they need it).

- Instore donations

This is a new addition to the easyfundraising scheme. Supporters register their debit card with easyfundraising and then whenever they make a purchase with it at participating stores, it will generate a donation. More and more retailers are signing up to this so it is worth investigating, especially if your school is in an urban area where parents are more likely to go shopping in the stores or buy coffee regularly. If someone bought a coffee on their way to work every day from a participating retailer a 5% of their yearly coffee spend could be a significant amount of money!

-Free donations

There is a section on the easyfundraising website that has details of ways that supporters can generate free donations for their cause. They are largely doing online surveys, registering with websites, signing up for mailing lists or agreeing to take free trials. They change every week so it is well worth the PTA admin keeping an eye on it so that if a new opportunity that would appeal to their supporters is listed, they can post the link and encourage people to participate.

-Referring other good causes

This is a fantastic way of raising more money and helping other good causes too. If another good cause signs up to easyfundraising via your PTA's referral link (on the easyfundraising website) then easyfundraising will pay your PTA 20% of what the new cause that you referred raises in its first year from online shopping donations. This is in addition to what the new cause earns so it does not "cost" them anything- it is an additional payment from easyfundraising as a bonus for referring a new good cause to them. Because you only earn the 20% for the first year that the new cause is registered, you do need to keep an eye out for new causes if you want to maintain this extra fundraising scheme- keep asking parents if they are involved with other local good causes e.g. brownies, cubs, playgroups, local animal rescues, churches etc. and if they are would the cause be interested in joining. I always used to encourage referrals with our PTA by offering to help them get set up on the site, get the first new supporters on board and be there to answer any questions they might have. You have to make sure that the new organisation joins using the special link, and the PTA admin will get an email to notify them when a new good cause joins from their referral link. If you are a small school in particular this can be a great way to boost what you raise, especially if you can get a larger organisation involved via your referral- their 20% might be 50% of what your smaller organisation earns!

eBay

eBay can raise money, but it is time consuming so you need a willing volunteer or two and preferably ones that like doing things on eBay. If you are going to sell things on eBay you need stock- you can either sell donated items or if you can think of something that you can sell lots of brand new you can buy in stock to sell.

Tips

- You can register your PTA as a charity with eBay / Paypal if it is a registered charity. This is good because it lets sellers choose to donate up to 100% of their list price to the PTA and eBay do not charge fees on the amount donated to the charity. It also means that anyone can choose to donate a proportion of the amount they sell items to the PTA as people can choose to donate to a charity and select the one they want from a list. This gives the potential to publicise this and ask that if anyone is selling on eBay that they consider giving a proportion of their sales to the PTA.
- PTAs can also sell on eBay themselves and not have to pay any fees.
- The registration process is straightforward and quick. The payment to the charity works differently to normal eBay listings, with Paypal making payments to charities once a month.

- Look up "eBay for Charity" in the Help section of eBay for further details on how to do this.
- If you decide to sell donated items on eBay, you could use suitable items that have been donated for other fundraisers such as BagstoSchool or Jumble Sales / Car Boot Sales. It is a good idea to let people know that this may happen to their items and give them the chance to specify that they do not want this to happen to anything they donate.
- You can search on eBay for "Sold Listings" to see if it is worth trying to sell something on eBay- it is better to sell a few well chosen eBays that go for a worthwhile sum than listing lots of items that either sell for 99p or don't sell at all. If anything that you choose doesn't sell you can just put it back into BagstoSchool for next time or save it for the next Jumble Sale (storage permitting).
- When selling on eBay- if an item is big or heavy it may well be easier to specify local pickup only to save having to post it. If you are posting sold items be sure you are charging enough postage on the listing to cover the postage cost or your volunteer seller will be out of pocket.

Fairs- Christmas / Easter / Summer

The School Fair, whether that is for Christmas, Easter, Summer or any other occasion is usually a major contributer to the funds a PTA raises in a year. Because of this, and the number of elements involved in holding a successful Fair, they have their own chapter after this A-Z.

Fashion Show

Fashion Shows can be a lucrative and fun way to raise money for the PTA. You can run the whole event yourselves (sourcing clothes / models etc) or you can get specialist companies to come in. The specialist companies are an attractive option as they bring lots of brand new clothes from reputable retailers at highly discounted prices, often provide the service for free and also often donate a voucher for you to raffle off. The PTA has to provide the venue and willing volunteers to be the models. The company can provide the service for free because it makes its money from selling the clothes. The PTA makes most of the money from ticket sales but could also run a raffle on the night or have a tombola / cake stall etc to boost the funds raised.

Tips:

- Contact the companies well in advance to find out when you can have a fashion show as they can book up far in advance.
- Check the terms and conditions of the companies you are looking at such as what they charge, what clothes they bring etc to decide which company you want to use, as well as checking they will cover your location.
- Consider where you want to hold the fashion show- is school suitable or would a village hall or similar be better. Check the venue is available on the date that you have booked the fashion show.
- Make sure you have enough people willing to be models before you book the event.
- Choose your ticket price so that it makes you a profit but isn't so expensive that it puts people off- many PTAs sell them for around £5 each.
- Consider how to publicise the event to maximise your ticket sales as this is your main source of income for this event, and also the more people there the more fun it will be. You could put information in the weekly bag, post on social media and see if you can get a mention in the local paper to encourage people from the wider community to come. If there are any noticeboards locally that you could put posters up this would be another way to build awareness of the event.

Fathers Day / Mothers Day Shops

These may not be huge fundraisers but they are very popular with the children. The PTA charges a fee per child to let them choose a present for their parent / carer for Father's or Mother's Day which they can then also write a gift tag for so that they have their own present to give to the parent on Father's or Mother's Day.

Tips:

- Send a flier home to all parents at least two weeks before the event informing parents that it will be held and asking that they return the reply slip with the cost per child (£2-£3 as a suggested amount).
- It is nice to give the children a selection of gifts to choose from. Buying online is good because it means things get delivered rather than having to go and get them, and depending on retailer you could purchase using easyfundraising if you use it which will earn a bit of cashback for the PTA on the amount spent. If you are a large school and therefore buying large quantities of presents it might be a large spend! Having a selection of say six different gifts for children choose from gives them a good choice but means you are only having to identify six different gift items. Always buy a few extra items so that the last children through are not forced to take the last one without having a choice. Hopefully you will have raised enough to cover the cost of a few extra of each item, and the extra items can be used as prizes in future events.
- Some item suggestions are: Chocolates (Homebargains sells multipacks of Thorntons or similar chocolates for about £1 a packet which are always popular for both Mothers and Fathers Day).

Mothers Day: A shower gel / bubble bath / lip balm / handcream /plant (if you can find them cheaply and have a green fingered volunteer you could get someone to plant bulbs in pots so they are nearly flowering by the time of the event- this needs a bit of advance planning though but is a lovely gift if you can do it).

Fathers Day: Shower gel / socks / car shampoo or other car related items / gloves (buy joblots of either cheaply off eBay)

- If you have a parent who is willing to donate items from their work this is great if they can provide enough of them as it means you have more money per item for the other gifts
- When buying the items consider how to save money- if you can find things on special offer such as half price or buy one get one free that always helps, especially if you could be buying 30-40 or more of each thing depending on the size of your school. Do check that the price per item is reasonable. Superdrug's website is good for special offers.
- If you happen to have a parent who is an Avon representative, see if they could source you some items. You will need to ask them far enough in advance to get time to put the order in and for it to arrive, but you could ask if there is anything suitable in the Avon catalogue that the Reps get (as well as the one they give out to customers they get another one just for reps) which has clearance offers- if you could get them to source you bubble bath at £1 each for a massive bottle that will be good for you, and they will be happy as it will boost their sales even if they don't make money on it, and if the parents like the bubble bath or whatever the item is enough they may gain a new customer or two.
- Make absolutely sure that whoever you have tasked to do the shopping for this event understands that they have a budget to keep to and unless you have decided to run it as a break even event, that this will be less than the amount you are charging per child. If they don't you run the risk that they will spend the amount you are charging per child which will make for nice gifts but

won't raise you any money! Also make sure they understand they have to keep the receipts for their purchases so that they can reclaim the money from the PTA. If you are charging £2.50 per child a budget of £1-1.25 per item is reasonable as you will also have to wrap the gifts and provide gift tags. You can be flexible in that if you find one item at 85p each then you can afford to spend a bit more on one of the other items.

- This event can be done quickly and efficiently if you do the following:
  - o Prewrap all the presents except one of each so that the children can see the sample. This saves an enormous amount of time at the event.
  - o See if the school will allow children to write their gift tags as a writing exercise in class, this also will save lots of time
  - o If you can run the event in the school hall, have tables laid out with the presents on them with the sample at the front so it is easy for the children to see and pick the present they want. Don't put all of the wrapped presents out at once though as it is fairer to stagger it a bit so that the first children through don't take all of the most popular item and leave the last children through with no choice.
  - o If the children have their prewritten gift tags with them they just take the present they want and a PTA helper sellotapes the gift tag to the gift (making sure the child's name is clear and if not putting it on). Then the children put the present with tag into a bag which is given to the class teacher to distribute the presents to children at hometime.
  - o Get classes to come through one at a time if possible so that the children are not too crowded and to prevent any mixups with the wrong presents going into the wrong bags.

If you follow the tips above you will be able to run the event in a quarter of the time or even less compared to if you were wrapping presents as they were chosen and getting the children to write the gift tags there and then. This is a much more efficient way to do it which is good for the PTA and the school will like it as it causes much less disruption to them.

- Check that school is happy for this event to be run. If a school sadly has a child who has lost a parent they may feel that the event is not appropriate as no one would want to cause upset to a child who has lost a parent.
- Also consider what your policy is for children that haven't had payment sent for them to participate. If it is just a handful of children in the school, many PTAs would let them participate rather than exclude them from the event- this is something your PTA will need to decide.

Film Night

These can be a fun way to raise money. However you do need to make sure that you comply with the necessary licence requirements so that you are not infringing copyright by showing a film without having the licence. The cost of the licence depends on whether you are charging entry to see the film, or whether you are allowing people to come and see the film but are charging for refreshments as well as whether you are just running the event for the school population or to the wider community.

If you are a member of PTA-UK, they have extensive information about how to organise a film night and obtaining the correct licence on their website. If you are not a member, it is strongly recommended that you research carefully to ensure that if you are running a film night you purchase the correct sort of licence for the type of event you wish to have, and also the film you want to show.

Gift Aid

If your PTA is a registered Charity in the UK it can register to claim Gift Aid. This means it can claim back tax on donations made by supporters who are registered with the scheme- 25p for every £1 donated. Whether this is worth doing for your PTA depends on your parent population- if many of them are in reasonably well paid jobs then it will be worth looking at as potentially you could claim a significant amount of money back. If your schools is perhaps in a less affluent area with less parents in well paid work then it may not be such an urgent priority for your PTA. It is definitely worth looking at though as it can yield a significant amount of money.

Tips:

-   Donors will need to have paid at least as much tax as you are wanting to claim back.
-   Donors must fill in a Gift Aid declaration giving your PTA permission to claim the Gift Aid on their donations
-   You must be able to prove that your PTA is a registered charity
-   You must be able to provide detailed records of donations received as part of your claim
-   You have up to 4 years to claim Gift Aid from when the donation was made
-   If your claim is successful the money will be paid directly into your PTA's bank account
-   See the gov.uk website (Gift Aid) for more details on the scheme and what is needed to make a claim

Grant applications

PTAs work so hard to raise money for their school. However, many overlook a funding source that could potentially make a massive difference to what they can achieve in a year-applying for a grant. If your PTA is a registered charity, there are many charitable trusts that are awarding grants. You might have to apply for a few grants before you are successful but imagine how many cakes you would have to sell from a cake stall to equal a grant of a few hundred pounds or more! It is definitely worth looking into as up to two billion pounds is given away in the form of grants every year in the UK. If you can manage to secure funding for that £5000 play equipment you have been fundraising for it will be worth the time researching and applying for grants.

Tips

- Do your research when deciding which grants to apply for. There is a lot of information available on the internet, although many of these are subscription based. If you are a member of PTA-UK, they have resources for members wanting to apply for grants, including access to their grants data base for a certain amount of time.
- When applying for grants- it is better to do a few really good applications that are tailored to each organisation that you are applying for then writing hundreds of begging letters as the higher quality applications have a far better chance of success.
- Check and double check the criteria for each organisation that you are applying to so that you are sure that your application meets them all or your application is unlikely to be successful.
- Plan in advance so that you are not rushing to get an application done at the last minute before a closing date. They do take a bit of time to put together but are worth the effort if you are successful!
- You will probably find that many grants you apply for need to be for a specific project so choose carefully to find the ones that sound closest to what you are raising money for e.g. outdoor play area etc to maximise your chance of success.

Ice Cream Sales

Selling ice creams after school- a fun way to raise money that the children really enjoy. You can make enough of a mark up on supermarket own icecream to make it worthwhile without having to make the icecreams too expensive.

Tips:

-Plan the dates in advance so that you can get agreement from the school and set up a rota for volunteers to run the stall.

- Depending on your school you could run it every Friday during the summer term, or just for special occasions such as when school is breaking up for half term / the holidays. Parents have been known to complain about it being too often if they have to hang around whilst the children are eating their icecreams if they won't let them eat them in the car but you will know your parent population best and whether this is going to be an issue for your PTA. You could always run it once and see how it goes before you decide how often to run it.

- If you have sufficient freezer space to store large quantities of icecream you can order it in bulk via internet supermarket shopping. This is convenient as you don't have to go and get it, and they will deliver it to you in their special vans to keep it frozen until it is delivered. If you don't have storage space for lots of icecream, see if you can get a PTA member to add it to their weekly supermarket internet delivery- if someone happens to get one regularly on the morning of the day you are running the icecream sales this can work really well if they don't mind bringing it to school.

- You can get supermarket own icecream cones for 25p each, so selling them for 50p each will double your money and there is no hassle putting icecream in cones yourself, although this way might make a bit more profit.

- See if you can find out from school how many children they have that might not be able to icecream due to lactose intolerance or other similar reasons. Consider purchasing a suitable alternative such as ice lollies so that these children are not excluded but buy a few more than you think you need in case the other children choose those.

- Have a contingency plan in place in case you have icecream left over that needs to be stored until the following icecream event or if you have to postpone an icecream sale day because of wet weather.

- Have a way to keep icecreams frozen during the icecream sale itself and if you have to take any away afterwards- cool boxes work well.

International Day / Event

These are a fun day for the children which allow them to learn about another country and can be a nice change from the usual PTA fundraising events. See if school is learning about another country, or if the children are studying a particular language and see if school would like to run a themed day that the PTA can tie in with.

Tips:

-Let the children come in non uniform for the day and ask that they come in clothes associated with the country that the day is themed for

- Consider having a cake stall with cakes appropriate to the themed country (e.g. croissants for France, strudel for Germany).

- You could run a family supper evening in the theme of the chosen country- music / food etc and charge a flat rate per person to include the meal.

Jubilee (or similar) day

It is nice for the children to celebrate something of historical importance like the Queen's Jubilee as it lets them feel involved with something that they will be hearing about on the television or in the newspapers. It also gives the opportunity for them to learn a bit about what they are celebrating so for the Queen's Jubilee they might learn about the monarchy / history. You could run it as a normal school disco but theme it to tie in with whatever it is you are celebrating. Tips:

- Obviously you will need to tailor the event to what you are celebrating but using the Queen's Jubilee as an example you could do:
   o Union Jack bunting / decorations for the hall
   o Cupcakes themed in red / white / blue / union jacks (depending on how artistic your cupcake makers are feeling!) as the children's snack at the event.
   o Suggest that the children come dressed in red / white / blue
- You could do nail painting and / or facepainting and offer designs that tie in with the theme e.g. red / white / blue for the Queen's Jubilee example

Jumble Sales

Jumble sales are great fun- people get to clear out all their unwanted clutter and can pick up some bargains! They can be lucrative fundraisers too

Tips:

- Consider your venue- school or somewhere else like a village hall that is cheap to hire, has plenty of space and could attract members of the wider community if advertised well
- Create an event on Facebook for the Jumble Sale so that parents can invite friends and family (and Facebook will send them reminders about the event). Your event could also give details of how to donate unwanted items.
- Plan well in advance so that you have plenty of time to publicise the event- both to attract people to the event itself and to appeal for donations from the wider community as well as the school population
- Consider how you will ask for donations to be made: where and when are you asking people to drop it off to / have you got volunteers that would be willing to collect it from people / where will you store it before the event
- Charge a small entry fee for the jumble sale- 50p a person is small enough for people not to mind paying it but with enough people coming will add up to a reasonable amount
- Make sure you publicise the jumble sale to the wider community as many people enjoy coming to jumble sales- posters up in shop windows / on notice boards / listed in the events in the local paper (and a write up too if you're lucky) will all help with this.
- Boost the fundraising by selling simple refreshments: teas / coffees / soup and have a PTA cake stall
- Make sure you do a rota of the volunteers that you need (e.g. 4 for stalls, 2 for teas and coffees, 1 for the cake stall ; all at one hour slots so for a two hour event you need

two volunteers for each volunteer "slot" plus help setting up beforehand and clearing everything afterwards. If you make a rota and ask people to commit to their one hour hopefully it should be easier to find volunteers than if you are asking people to commit to help for the whole time plus setting up and clearing away.

- If you can get the majority of donations before the event, spend a little time arranging it all e.g. all toys together, a book section, clothes sorted into childrens / ladies / mens / shoes / bags and then bric a brac

- Make it easier for the volunteers and the customers by having prices displayed e.g. each item of clothing on this rail £1; small toys 50p each; medium toys £1 each; large toys £2 each. This means it will be quicker to sell things as customers won't have to ask the prices of everything they are interested in, and having rounded prices means it will be that bit easier to deal with the cash transactions.

- Half an hour or so before the Jumble Sale is due to finish, you could announce that everything left is being reduced to half price- you want to minimise what is left over at the end and this will hopefully provoke a last minute rush to buy more items from the people there.

- What will you do with any left over stock after the event? Some suggestions are:
    o Save any good condition and appropriate books for future PTA book stalls
    o If any large good condition items like toys see if you can sell them on the local Facebook advertising groups or eBay.
    o If you can book your jumble sale not too long before the next BagstoSchool collection, keep any leftover clothes / shoes / bags for that (you could remove any designer or other high value clothing items for sale on eBay if anyone is willing to do this for you)
    o Have a strategy for what you will do with the left over items, try to raise more money from them as above and then you could donate any other unwanted items that you have not

got a use for to a local charity shop so that another good cause benefits too

Ladies' Night

A chance for the Mums, Grans, Aunts and any other Ladies you can think of to come and have a nice relaxing evening shopping and maybe getting some pampering too! And can be a lucrative fundraiser for the PTA as well. Get the stalls to pay a small fee (£10 or so) and donate a prize for the raffle.

Tips:

- Again, decide your venue early on- you need to know this before you start publicising the event so that you can name the venue on the publicity as well as being able to plan how many stalls you can fit into the venue of your choice.
- You will probably want to get a variety of stalls at the event. These could include:
   o Local beauticians to do manicures / mini-facials hopefully at a discounted price as they will be keen to have so many potential customers
   o Head / feet massage stall
   o Eyebrow stall
   o Avon or similar- see if you have any parents who are reps for these, they would be happy to come and have a stall as potentially they could gain new regular customers as well as sell on the night
   o Jewellery stall
   o Nice stationary stall
   o Handbags / scarves / accessories
   o Tombola- perhaps with beauty / pampering related prizes, or wine is usually popular too depending on what prizes you can source

- o Raffle- if you can make up a hamper from the prizes donated by the other stall holders you can display it and sell raffle tickets for the raffle to be drawn at the end of the night.
- o If you decide to run this event in the Autumn term, you could consider marketing it as a Ladies Shopping Event and opportunity for people to do some Christmas shopping. You could then widen the type of stall you invite to the event to increase the shopping aspect rather than purely as a pamper event where Ladies can buy things for them.
- Sell tickets for the event- you could include a glass of wine and some nibbles in the cost (make sure you check licensing requirements where you are if you decide to do this).

Match funding

This is a fantastic but little utilised way of significantly increasing the amount of money that your PTA can raise. Essentially if you have a parent that works for a company who does match funding, their company could donate a sizeable amount of money to your PTA. Different companies have different criteria but a common way for them to work it is if their employee raises £x amount then they will match it (up to a maximum amount). So if you can have a parent in such a scheme helping on an event that raises £250 then potentially their employer could make an additional donation of another £250- doubling the amount that you raise.

Tips

- Your PTA will most likely need to be a registered charity in order to be eligible to apply for a match funding scheme.
- You need to know whether your parents work for

companies with match funding schemes! To find out you could:

- o Put in your annual parent questionnaire some questions asking which companies parents work for and if the parents know if they offer match funding schemes. It is important to ask which company they work for in case they don't know that the company offers such a scheme. Conversely a parent might work for a company that you do not know offers match funding but they know that it does.
- o Do a specific publicity drive asking for parents who work for known match funding companies to contact the PTA to let them know they work for them. They can then be approached to ask if they would apply for match funding.
- o Everyone is busy, but if you can tell a parent that potentially their helping out on a stall at an event could help raise the PTA hundreds of extra pounds they will hopefully be motivated to volunteer if they realise they can make such a big difference to the total amount raised.

- Some companies offer match funding / community schemes to local charitable causes where they do have to have an employee who is involved with the charity. This is common in banks particularly so it is worth seeing if the bank where you have your PTA bank accounts runs anything like this. Sometimes rather than granting money, companies like to be able to send employees to volunteer for a day- this could help save money by getting them to do work like garden clearing / painting and reduce the amount a project costs so you don't have to raise as much money for it.
- List of companies that have had match funding schemes (you will need to get any parents who work at these companies to confirm they are still running) is at back of book

Non Uniform Day

A mainstay of PTA fundraising! Children enjoy them and they can be very worthwhile for the PTA to run.

Tips:

- Check with school how often they are happy for you to run them- you don't want them to lose their novelty with the children or for parents to feel that they are being asked to donate for things too often. Every term or half term is probably enough.
- As well as non uniform days where the children just wear their own clothes you could hold themed non uniform days where children can dress up according to your them.
- You can either run non uniform days where the children are asked to bring a monetary donation with them in order not to wear their uniform (say £1) or you can ask children to bring a donation which the PTA can use for a future event. Consider which is more beneficial in terms of whether the PTA just wants the money raised from straight donations, or if they could use donations to get a higher return such as tombola / raffle prizes. In many cases it can be more cost effective to get children to bring in donations, particularly if you have an event planned and know what sort of prizes you need. If you can do a non-uniform day and ask for new items to be donated (most people have some new unused items around the house- whether unusued gifts or whatever) these can be really useful for tombola or raffle prizes.
- If you are a larger school, you could ask different year groups to bring in different donations. That way you can get enough prizes to run different types of stalls e.g. a tombola and a book stall by asking one year group to bring in books, another to bring in tombola prizes etc.
- Make sure you send out notification to parents a week or two before (the more notice the better, especially if

children are being allowed to dress up for a theme day as parents will want time to organise costumes) and remember to send out reminders via social media and the school's text message service if this is available to you.

Panto / Theatre trips

Many theatres offer PTAs the opportunity to block buy large numbers of tickets at discounted prices. The PTA can then sell the tickets to the children and their families- this can be a popular event as it means all the children and families from one school are seated together and it is a social occasion. You will find that these tickets are often for performances early on in the season such as pantomime tickets being in the first week or two of the pantomime's run.

Tips:

- Consider if you want to try and make a profit from the tickets or if you will sell them on at cost. Some PTAs are happy to sell the tickets at a small markup which gives them a profit but still allows parents to make a saving on the standard price of the tickets. Other PTAs feel that as many theatres are charities they do not want to make a profit on the back of a charity giving them a discount on tickets. Individual PTAs will need to decide how they feel about this.
- You will need to book your tickets and performance date well in advance. You may find that the theatre requires a percentage deposit on the tickets, with the balance payable once the final numbers are confirmed and the tickets bought by the PTA.
- Send notification out to parents well in advance of the date and ticket cost so that they have the chance to return the information slip with details of tickets they want and payment. Pantomime tickets can be expensive (even if discounted) for a whole family so if you can give

a few weeks notice this allows people to have another payday before having to send payment if required.

- It is helpful to have one or two volunteers working on this as their project so that they can administer it effectively. They will need to keep records of:
    o Who wants tickets and how many
    o Whether payment has been received (so they can chase up people who have expressed an interest but not yet paid when the final numbers need to be confirmed and the tickets paid for).
    o Payments made to the theatre- both the deposit and the balance (remember to take the deposit amount off the final amount payable once the total number of tickets required is known)
    o Ticket numbers allocated to families (they will need to seat families together so will have to work out where to place people according to the size of their party).
    o Use the theatre's seating plan to work out how to seat families together and allocate all of the tickets so that they are used without ending up with empty seats in the middle!
- Have a deadline at least a week before the performance in order to allow sufficient time to chase late payments, allocate the seating, pay for and collect the tickets and finally distribute them out.

Performance DVD

Some PTAs arrange for a school performance (often the Christmas performance but could work for any others too) to be filmed and then sell copies of the DVD to parents. This can be lucrative as families are likely to want to purchase a copy of their children performing, and often extra copies for other family members such as grandparents.

Tips:

- Firstly you must check with school if they are open to this idea. They may have children on roll who, for various reasons, cannot be photographed or filmed. This is often for safeguarding reasons so it is very important to check with the school if they are willing for this idea to be explored or if they are unwilling for school performances to be filmed and the recordings sold.
- If school is happy for the performances to be filmed, consider the logistics- have you got a parent who is good at filming who could be persuaded to do it? If you have someone with the necessary equipment then this could make it more viable in terms of cost.
- If you have got a parent who knows how to film (and hopefully has the necessary equipment) you will need to consider how the DVDs will be duplicated- can they do this if the PTA supplies the blank DVDs or would this need to be done by someone else.
- Calculate carefully the costs involved in producing the DVDs e.g. blank DVDs, the cases, producing the covers so that you can work out how much to sell them for to make a profit.
- If you don't have someone who can do the filming work for you, there are professional companies who will provide this service. You will need to research if there are any companies that can do this that will cover your area and how much they will charge. Some companies will do the filming and DVD production for a set fee, others come out to do the filming for free but then take the money from the DVD sales (so you would have to see if adding a mark up to the cost they charge was an option in order to make money from the exercise). Some companies will give a number of copies for free depending on how many are sold which could give some opportunity for profit if you can sell the ones you are given for free. The prices charged per DVD can be up to £18.95 each which is obviously a large amount of money for parents to pay, so it is important to research the costs involved carefully if you are considering

bringing a company in to do the filming.

- If you are going to bring a company in to film the performance, check if school wants the people they send to be DBS checked and if so find out if the companies that you are interested in have DBS checked staff.

Parental donations-

Some PTAs have schemes where parents can make a regular financial donation to the school PTA. This appeals in particular to those parents who may work long hours who lack the time to physically help with PTA events but who still wish to contribute to their PTA. Parents could make regular donations either by setting up a standing order with their bank to send the payments or by Payroll giving schemes if their employer runs them.

Tips:

- PTAs can give parents the opportunity to make a regular payment to the PTA by setting up a standing order to pay directly into the PTA bank account. If the PTA tells people they can do this, and provides the necessary form for them to fill in to set it up they may find they get some people signing up.
- You could encourage anyone who wants to set up a standing order to the PTA to also do a Gift Aid declaration (providing they are paying tax) which will immediately boost the amount of money the PTA gets from this scheme.
- Sample Standing Order and Gift Aid declaration forms are in the Sample template section of this book.
- Payroll giving schemes tend to be run by larger employers. They can be attractive to parents who want to donate regularly because they don't pay tax on the money that they are donating, and because the money comes straight out of their wages.

- The PTA can't set up a Payroll giving scheme- this is done by employers for their employees to opt in to and specify the charity they wish to donate to. However you could do a publicity drive or put in your new parents information pack that parents are very welcome to choose your PTA if they wish to start using their employer's Payroll giving scheme.
- PTAs have to be registered charities in order to be eligible to receive money under a Payroll giving scheme.
- Gift Aid can't be claimed on money donated through a Payroll giving scheme (because the money hasn't been taxed).

Plant Sales

A slightly different fundraising idea- but one that can be a good fundraiser and popular with parents and children. If the PTA can find a large nursery that is willing to discount for bulk orders (or one that is reasonably priced so that the PTA can add a mark up to their prices to make a profit), they could consider selling bedding plants in the spring. Bedding plants are inexpensive, and people like buying them as an easy way to brighten up their gardens so it is possible to get a worthwhile number of orders.

Tips:

- Research local garden centres / nurseries to find one that offers suitable plants at suitable prices (or will give you a discount for bulk buying). One that will deliver the plants to you is desirable as the plants are delicate to transport and take up quite a lot of room so if you can't get a nursery to deliver you may need to see if you can find a volunteer with a van to collect it.
- Make a list of the plants you want to offer- although tempting to offer lots of different plants, it is easier in terms of sorting orders and dealing with the collections not to offer too many different sorts of plants. Let the

nursery suggest what might be suitable.

- See if the nursery will provide you with pictures of the plants when they are flowering so you can create a post on social media for parents to have a better idea of what they are choosing (you could put them on a flier but that would be dependent on being able to colour copy the fliers).

- Work out how much you want to charge for each different type of plant by looking at the price you will be charged for each one plus delivery cost if applicable before deciding what your mark up will be. You want to make a profit but keep the price attractive to parents if possible. Making the prices you charge a round number makes it easier in terms of totalling orders and taking payments.

- Consider the timing for doing your Plant Sale- you want to have it early enough so that people can get the plants into their gardens to look nice and flower, but not so early that there is still a risk of frost which could kill the plants once in peoples' gardens. If you happen to be having a spring fair, cake stall or car boot sale and your plant collection day is shortly before any of these events you could consider ordering a few extra plants to be sold at the event.

- Make an order form for parents to fill in and return with their payment. Payment in advance makes it much easier on the day of collection so that you are not having to take money as well as make sure everyone gets the correct orders. It also means that you are only ordering what is needed and won't lose money if people forget to collect their plants.

- Find out from the nursery how much notice they need to provide the plants that you are ordering and factor this into your planning of when you will send the information and order form out to parents- you want to give parents a week or two to look at the information and decide what they want, and probably a week for you to collate the returned orders before submitting the PTA's order to the nursery.

- Make sure you double check each order you receive to ensure that the correct payment has been sent with it so that you have time to rectify any errors that may have been made prior to collection day.
- Keep all the order forms. For the day of collection you will definitely need a list of all the people who have ordered and what they have ordered, and it would be sensible to have a copy of the order for parents to take away with their plants so that they can see they have the correct order (if you have recorded all the details for your list you could let them take back their original order form). Keep them alphabetically so they are easy to find on the day of collection.
- Consider where you will have the plants on collection day and how you will organise them. You could have all the plants divided up by type and then as people arrive to collect their plants you can gather the plants they have ordered using their original order form which you can then give to them along with their plants. Or you could put out all the orders already sorted with the order forms with them so you can see who they are for. You would probably want the orders in alphabetical order so that it is easy to find the right one.
- Make sure parents know there is a process to follow for them to collect their order so that they don't go diving in to grab the plants they ordered and risk disrupting your system.
- See if you can source suitable containers (shallow boxes) for people to take their orders away in- this is make it easier for you as people won't be struggling to carry all their plants away so will be dealt with more quickly, and gives you something to attach individual order forms to if you decide to make up all the orders in advance. The quicker and easier you can make the collection process for parents the more likely they are to order again if you decide to do the event in subsequent years (and it is easier on the PTA volunteers too).
- Have a plan in case it rains on collection day. Will you be in a hall or outside? If you are meant to be outside is

there anywhere undercover you could be and if not how will you make sure that the order forms don't get wet and become illegible.

- If you decide to order a few extra plants for sale at forthcoming PTA events, make sure you know who is going to store them and that they will be happy and able to look after them (ie keep them alive and looking nice) before the event you want to sell them at.

Promise Auction (silent or live)

Promise Auctions can raise a phenomenal amount of money. They are hard work and do take a lot of planning but can definitely be worth it in terms of the money raised and the satisfaction of having run a fun event. You can run an auction that is just items that you are selling off, but adding the element of "Promises" adds variety to what people can bid on and seems to make the events more popular. Some of the "Promises" can provoke real bidding wars depending on what they are! Because Promise Auctions are so time consuming in terms of organising and securing prize donations, many PTAs decide to run them every other year. This also maintains the novelty and popularity of the event so this is worth bearing in mind when deciding how often to run them.

Tips:

- There are two commonly used auction methods: Silent or Live. You need to decide which of these you want to use for your auction.
- Silent: This is where people can view all of the lots in advance- you can issue a catalogue and then also have them available to view at school. These tend to work well run in conjunction with another event that you have large numbers of people attending such as a Summer Fair or Christmas Fair (then people might want to bid on

items as Christmas presents) or even a school performance if your school is willing and you can find a suitable location to put the auction display where people will see it.

- o Have as many items on display as possible as people are more likely to want to buy things that they can see. If a lot is for a service rather than an item you could still have a big picture relating to that together with the text (e.g. a big pile of freshly ironed clothes to go with an hour's ironing).
- o Make sure your auction catalogue is distributed well in advance of the auction date to give parents the chance to look at it. Make it clear that if parents can't be there on the night they can submit bids in advance (give a firm deadline and time for this) and make it easier for them by including a form at the back of the catalogue for them to return with the details of what they are bidding for and how much should they wish to do this.
- o Make it clear in the catalogue if some items will have a reserve that means if they don't reach this in bids they will not be sold.
- o Decide how you will get people to bid at the actual auction itself. Do you want people to fill in slips for their bids and submit them to the PTA who can then collate them in order to find out the winning bidder for each item? If so do you want slips for each lot or one slip per bidder. Or would you prefer people write their bids on a whiteboard for everyone to see? (this can either encourage competition if people see they are being outbid on something or discourage bidding because people don't want other people to see how much they are bidding- you will need to decide which system you think is best for your auction and PTA).
- o Have a firm closing time for bids. You will need

to build in a bit of time between the time to stop accepting bids and when you will announce the winning bidders to allow you to collate all the bids and determine who the winning bidder for each item is. This is easier to manage if you are running the auction alongside another event, if you are just running a silent auction you will need to think about how you will "entertain" people in the time that you are doing this or if you think it is better to end the event once you have stopped taking bids and inform people the next day. Informing people the next day means contacting them all though which could make it more time consuming afterwards.

- Live: This is where you run the auction as a specific event where you want as many parents and family members to attend (the more people attending the more potential bidders you have).
    o Consider if you want to run the live auction as a specific stand alone event or at the end of another event which will have large numbers of attendees already there such as the school performance. The number of lots that you have and how long you think the auction will take is a factor in this, as is how many people you think you will be able to get to come to the auction as a standalone event rather than having them already there.
    o As for silent auctions, make sure that the auction catalogue is distributed a week or two in advance and give parents who can't be there on the night the ability to place bids in advance.
    o You will need a good auctioneer! Have you any parents that would be good at this? Would the headteacher be suitable and willing? For a church school what about the vicar? It needs

to be someone who is comfortable talking in front of large numbers of people, can create and maintain a good atmosphere and who can also keep track of the items they are ordering and what the bids on them are (so they are taking bids on the right item and making sure that all bids are taken before they say SOLD!).

o Will you be offering refreshments at the auction? Offering parents a glass of wine can be worthwhile in terms of encouraging them to bid more! Or will you be selling refreshments. If you are offering or selling alcohol be sure to check the licensing requirements where you are.

o This will largely depend on whether you are putting the auction on after the school performance or as a standalone event, but consider what the intentions are for children. If the auction is after the school performance, they will probably want to come and join their parents and can encourage them to bid on lots that they want their parents to win. If the auction is a standalone event you need to decide if you don't mind if people bring their children or if you want the auction as a parents only event. This can work well in terms of adults having a social event and being able to concentrate on the auction. The trouble with parent only events is that it means that parents need to arrange chidcare- could the PTA put on a crèche in a different part of the school so parents don't need to worry about finding (and paying for) childcare? This could encourage people to come if they are getting an adult social occasion where they can bring their children with them to go to the crèche and means they won't be spending money on childcare. A crèche will need some organising so it is not something to take on lightly but it is worth considering.

- o Have a PTA volunteer whose job it is to record how much each lot sells for and who to. It is essential that this information is recorded correctly. They could either write down on the catalogue or design their own form to record this. Consider where they should be seated so that they can get this information- next to the auctioneer may be the best place so they can clarify with them if needed.

- o Have something for each auction lot that the winning bidder can take with them once payment has been received. Obviously for an actual item they can take that when it is paid for. But for "Promises" e.g. an hours babysitting by Mrs Brown you will need to create a voucher for the parent so that they know they have got all the items they won and so that the prize isn't given to the wrong person by mistake. It also means the winning bidders have the details they need to use the prize once they have it without coming back to the PTA to find out how they need to use it (if you have the winning bidders of 30 "Promises" all coming back to you to find out how to use their prizes this will be time consuming to sort out- make sure all winning bidders get all the information they need when they pick up their prize).

- o Consider setting up a system so that you have all the vouchers in envelopes ready for the auction and ordered by lot number. Then it isn't too time consuming to record the winning bidder's name on the envelope once you have confirmed who they are and this makes it much easier when people come to pay and collect their items.

- o Decide how you are going to run payment for

auction items. Will you take payment on the night (so people can take their item away with them there and then). If you are taking payment on the night you will need to have a float. Or will you give people a set deadline to make payment (in which case you wouldn't release the item to them until payment had been made). How will you deal with people that don't pay by the deadline? You will need to have good record keeping in place so that you always know who won which items, and which have been paid for and who you need to chase for payment. Having a receipt book especially for the Promise Auction so you can record payments made and give parents a receipt (and you keep a copy) can be helpful for knowing who has paid.

- Whichever type of auction you decide to have, you need to plan it well in advance so that you have time to write out to potential prize donors and get their responses (and hopefully prizes). These will need to be listed in the catalogue that you need to produce with all the auction lots which takes time to do so the earlier that work can be started on this the better.
- Sourcing donations:
  - o Write out to all parents / post on social media to ask if anyone has anything they would like to donate- either personally or via their business or employer. Parents may have connections either personally or through their employment or businesses that could enable them to get some "money can't buy" prizes donated for the auction.
  - o Write out to local businesses. If PTA members know any local businesses personally get them to approach them as they are more likely to be successful if they already have a good relationship with a potential donor

o Things that sell well at auction are things that are unusual and would be difficult or impossible to get hold of normally- so if any PTA member or parent knows any chefs for example, could they be persuaded to do a cooking demonstration / lesson / cook a meal for a family (or do you have any chefs as parents who could be persuaded to donate their time for something like this). Or if any parents or PTA members have any contacts with celebrities of any sort could they be persuaded to donate something to help the school- signed memorabilia / tickets for a performance and the opportunity to meet them afterwards etc.

o If you are writing out to national companies to ask for donations, do this well in advance as often they receive hundreds or more requests a year- some companies allocate a number of items to give out to charities but once they have been used for the year that it is until the following year.

o Be imaginative! I secured a wonderful donation from a local car dealership for our PTA once as I had noticed that there was a particular model of car that was very popular with parents at our school. I got all the parents who owned the cars to line their cars up in the car park so that I could send a photo to the dealership who sold that particular car with the letter asking if they would consider making a donation. This encouraged the dealership to donate to us because it was a bit different from the usual run of the mill request for donations (when I collected their donation the manager told me that they received hundreds of requests and although they donated what they could they had to refuse most of them. He said they donated to us because we had made a real effort in taking the picture and of course they could see that a large number of their customers were parents at the school). If you can make your donation request stand out from all the other donation requests that a company receives, you have a better chance of getting a donation from them.

o   Promises- see what you can get parents to donate in the way of a "promise". This can be really whatever people can think of and are willing to offer, but some examples are:

- An hours ironing
- An hours cleaning
- Dog walking
- 2 hours babysitting (this tends to go for more if it is a known childcare professional, and even better one from the school who is offering this).
- Coming to your house to cook you and your family dinner (anyone can offer this but if it is a parent who is known to be a good cook or even better a chef obviously it will be more in demand so raise more money).
- 2 hours gardening help
- Slave for a day (or however long the person is willing to volunteer for)
- Decorating help (especially if the volunteer is a painter and decorator)
- Man with a van
- Car wash and valet
- 3 hour decluttering session
- Photo shoot (the more well known the photographer the better)
- Portrait
- Half a dozen fresh eggs a week from x parent's home bred free ranging chickens for a month
- Homebaking (if you have a parent who

is known for their amazing and not very often made cakes then if you can persuade them to offer one of their cakes for auction that can result in a real bidding war!). Or if you have any professional cake makers that would be willing to donate a promise to make a cake for the widding bidder of their auction that would also be a great promise auction item.

- Anything relating to someone's special skill such as a language lesson, music lesson, sporting lesson, sewing lesson, proof reading, CV writing, help with doing a job application form. Also hard to obtain or expensive expertise from a professional such as conveyancing- have you got any specialist solicitors; or in an area with high demand for school places if you are running the auction at a time where your Year 6 parents (for a primary school PTA) are gearing up for appealing for Secondary School places do you have a parent who is an expert in School Appeals who could offer an hours advice in helping parents prepare their case. Or advice around accountancy, tax or setting up a new business might also be in demand. This is another example of where knowing where your parents work / what they do professionally can be useful as this can give ideas of where you could approach parents to see if they would be willing to offer a prize connected with their professional skills that would be in demand (i.e. raise a lot of money) at auction.
- Anything relating to someone's special

skill as above but if you can find someone famously well known for their special skill e.g. sporting or music personalities who is willing to offer a lesson in it then that hopefully will raise lots of money as it would be one of those "money can't buy" things that people get carried away bidding on at auction

- Holiday accommodation- if you are lucky enough to have a parent willing to offer a weekend or longer at their holiday house / caravan etc this can raise a lot of money
- A private tour around..... (if someone works at a well known tourist attraction and is allowed to donate this that can be popular. Even more popular would be the chance to get a tour round somewhere well known that the public can't usually get to see)

- Keep accurate records of who has donated prizes / promises and make sure that everyone that has donated something, whether a parent, private individual or business gets a thank you letter from the PTA for their donation. You could tell them in the letter how much the auction raised in total so that they feel their donation contributed to something worthwhile. It is only polite to send a thank you, and if you want to run another auction in a year or two they will be more likely to donate again if they remember getting a thank you from last time they donated.

- For parents offering promises, be mindful that they need to keep them! 99% of parents will without question, but it is worth considering how to ensure that all of them do, particularly if donated by a parent who will be leaving the school at the end of the year- could an expiry date be issued to their promise and the parent reminded that they need to keep it before they leave? This is a tricky one as you don't want to annoy parents who have volunteered, but at the same time you do not want a parent paying for a promise that they then cannot "redeem". It is worth considering so that if there is a problem you have an idea of how you would deal with it, whether by reminding the person who donated the promise that the winning bidder paid £x for it and they are expecting to be able to redeem it, or if that is unsuccessful ultimately you may have to consider refunding the amount paid. Hopefully this won't be an issue but it is worth thinking about in case it does come up.

Quiz Night

Quiz nights are a good social event for parents. They can also do well as fundraisers.

Tips:

- Where will you hold the quiz night? At school or somewhere else? School means no venue hire costs but means it will need preparing after school and ensuring everything is tidied away again for use the next day (if on a week night). Depending on numbers of people you think might come you could see if a local pub would let you use a private room there.
- If you are thinking about using a local pub, see if they will let you have a private room and maybe donate some prizes to give to the winner (so you don't have to pay for prizes).
- If you are going to a pub that regularly runs quiz nights, you could see if they are willing to run the whole thing for you- this could be an easy way to do the event as you would provide the entrants and the pub would provide the venue, (hopefully) the prizes and all refreshments would be available to buy without the PTA having to organize them. There will be less money to be made but it would be an easier introduction to having a quiz night if

you haven't had one before. If the event goes well, you could look at holding it in a different venue the next time to give the PTA the opportunity to sell (and make money on) refreshments but you would have to make sure you complied with the licensing requirements to do this if you were selling alcohol.

- You will make money by entry fees for people wanting to do the quiz (do you want people to enter themselves individually or as teams or give them the option to do both and the PTA can arrange sole entrants into teams?).
- You could also run a raffle on the night to boost the money raised.
- You really need the Headteacher to be doing the quiz in a team from the school. This will make parents want to enter for the chance to beat the school team in the quiz and make it more competitive on the night.
- As for all events, you need to book your venue and send out information sheets out well in advance. Making it payment in advance saves having to take payment on the night and means that you know the people that have entered are more likely to come because they have already paid.
- Unless the pub can supply one, you will need to write your quiz for the night. See if any PTA members goes to pub quizzes so that they can advise (or write it for you!) as they will have a good idea of how many questions to have. You will also need a quiz master / mistress (if the Headteacher doesn't want to do the quiz perhaps they could do this but you do need at least one team of teachers doing the quiz if possible).

Raffles

Another mainstay of PTA fundraising! This is because they can be run at little cost and can generate large amounts of money in return. People like entering raffles for the chance to win something at small outlay so they tend to be popular.

Tips:

- Christmas raffles have been covered in their own section as they can do particularly well and can be worked round the Christmas Fair and Christmas performances but read the tips for them in case they are helpful for any other raffles you want to run.
- As for Christmas raffles, your PTA needs to have the Lottery and Gaming Licence to be able to run a raffle
- If you want to run a raffle you need to think about the following points:
  o You need to decide when you want to run your raffle. Can you tie it in with any other school events? (to give the opportunity to sell tickets to people at the events).
  o Selling raffle tickets at parent assemblies at school is a good way to boost ticket sales (if school doesn't mind this being done).
  o Where will you get the prizes? Can you ask for donations from parents or outside businesses / organisations. If from outside businesses / organisations you can offer publicity in return for the prize if you think that will improve your chances of getting donations.
  o Is the raffle going to be a one day only raffle such as on a cake stall for your "showstopper cake" or one that will be run over a period of time? If it is a one day raffle then you could use cloakroom tickets to sell, if it is to be run over a longer period of time then you could consider getting tickets printed for it.
  o If you are selling tickets at any events make sure your volunteers have a float and a supply of pens so that each ticket stub has the buyer's name and contact info (phone number) written on it to let them be contacted if they win a prize.
  o Decide how and where the raffle will be drawn- if you are running the raffle over a period of time, if you can tie it in with a large

event you could have the raffle drawn there (and this lets you try to encourage last minute ticket sales before the draw). If it is a one day only raffle make sure you tell buyers when it will be drawn so that they know when to expect the phone call if they are a winner!

- o Make sure you have a suitable container to put the ticket stubs in to draw the winning raffle tickets. A bucket is fine for one day only raffles, you might want something more glamourous (and bigger) for raffles that are done over a longer period of time.
- o If doing a raffle over a period of time, as for Christmas Raffles, make sure you don't leave folding the ticket stubs til the last minute as this can be quite time consuming if you have sold lots of tickets.

Recipe Books

Recipe books can be a nice way to raise money that involves parents and children. Parents like to buy the book, especially if their recipe is in the book!

Tips:

- Recipe books can take a bit of time to do from start to finish so need planning quite far ahead.
- How will you get recipes for the book?
  - o Ask all parents / children to submit their favourite recipe
  - o See if anyone knows any chef friends (or is a good customer at a local restaurant) to approach for them to write a recipe for the book.
  - o Ask the teachers to do their favourite recipes
  - o If there is a cookery club and there is a particular favourite thing that the children make there, see if that recipe can be put in

the book

- o If the children like a particular thing that they get for their school dinners, see if the staff can provide that recipe for the book e.g. Mrs Smith's Chocolate Brownies
- o Are there any parents who are known for their special cake or whatever that they always donate for cake stalls that people always want to buy because they are so nice? If so, could they be persuaded to give the recipe for the book? e.g. Mrs Tyson's secret Ginger Cake recipe finally revealed.

- Think about how you can increase awareness and anticipation for the book- can you run a competition for all the children to do a picture to be used as the cover? You could give all entrants a small prize and have a worthwhile prize for the winner. This motivates the children to take part and gets people talking about the forthcoming book.

- Decide how you will structure the book- this might depend on the types of recipe you get but you could have sections on Quick Snacks, Favourite Meals, Healthy Treats and Baking for example.

- Are you going to be having a cookery demonstration event? If so this is the perfect place to sell the recipe book but you will need to make sure that the book has the recipes used at the event or it won't tie in as well. You could make the cookery demonstration the launch event for the book.

- If you have any local restaurants (ideally the one where the chef at your cookery event works but if not see if there might be any others) see if you can tie in with them- could they supply a favourite recipe or two and in return you could print a 20% of your meal voucher at the back of the book for people to use? This would add another selling point to the book, especially if it is a popular restaurant. It would be good for the restaurant as it could encourage new potential customers to their restaurant.

- Think about the costs involved in producing the book. The traditional way of producing this type of book used by PTAs seems to be using spiral bound booklets containing the recipes with a laminated front cover. This way works perfectly well, but can be costly in terms of copying and time consuming to assemble the books. You could look at using Createspace or similar self publishing websites in order to produce a more professional looking end product. This involves registering with them and having to ensure your book is formatted to the template you choose but is a good way to get large quantities of books easily- once it is on the system you can just order more as you need them. If you choose to use this method, be aware that to take advantage of the cheaper "author copies" you can order directly through Createspace, you need to select the cheaper (i.e. slower) shipping options or it will increase the price per book significantly. As well as having the book as a professional looking book that you can just order on demand whenever you need more, this way gives the bonus that the book can be available on Amazon! This gives potential for widescale publicising of the book on social media and gives family members from further afield the ability to purchase the book if they like. See if you have a parent who already self publishes books so they know how to do it, if not it isn't that difficult to do as everything is done step by step and the website shows clear instructions throughout the process. Depending on whether you choose to have a book all in black and white, or with colour, the dimensions and how many pages which all influence the cost of the book, you could be looking at less than £2 per book including shipping which gives you plenty of room to add a decent markup and deliver a professional looking book to customers.
- Once you know how much it will cost to produce your book (including shipping costs if you have decided on the self publish option) you can decide what price to sell it at to give the PTA a reasonable profit without making it

so expensive that people don't want to buy it.

- Plan ahead and send out order forms to families to allow them to order books well in advance so you know how many books to order / make. If you are launching the book at a cookery event etc you will need to have extra copies available for sale there. If you are going to order the books from Createspace they can take 3-4 weeks to come if you want the cheapest shipping option so this needs to be planned well.

Recycling- phones / printer cartridges / CDs/ Ebay/ stamps / foreign coins

There are a multitude of ways that PTAs can make money from recycling. The biggest way is BagstoSchool for unwanted textiles which has its own section in this A-Z. However there are lots of other ways that recycling can benefit the PTA as well as educating children and families about recycling by setting up collections for whatever it is that you have decided to recycle.

Tips:

- Research the different recycling schemes available. Some ideas are listed below:
  - o Old mobile phones (tend to be worth more if they come with their original chargers)
  - o Printer cartridges (most printer cartridge recycling schemes are very specific about the types of cartridge they will accept- ensure that you make this very clear in the information that you give parents to try to minimise the number of incorrect cartridges you receive that will have to be removed from what you send away for recycling).
  - o CDs and DVDs- these are becoming an item that more and more people are recycling as the popularity of streaming services increases.

There are various schemes that you can recycle them with so research carefully before choosing so that you find the one that you think is most suitable for your PTA.

- o Stamps- you can get parents to collect stamps which you then send away and get paid for. You need a lot! But if you are a large school, or are prepared to keep hold of them for a while until you accumulate enough to send off then it could be a worthwhile exercise.
- o Foreign coins- something that most people who go away on foreign holidays seem to end up coming home with! Again, the size of your school can determine how viable this is to sign up for. If you can put out a flier before school breaks up for the summer holidays to tell people that the PTA is going to be collecting foreign coins when school starts again in September, hopefully people will remember and keep hold of any they bring back to donate once school starts. If you run the scheme over the course of the school year and send what you have collected in just before the school year ends, hopefully you will have collected enough to make a reasonable amount of money. You will need to decide where to store the coins as they come in through the year though!

- Other ways to make money from "recycling" unwanted items are eBay, jumble sales and car boot sales- they all have their own sections in this A-Z
- Whatever it is you decide to start recycling, bear in mind that you will need to write out to tell parents about it (and put on social media) and remind people from time to time that you are still collecting whatever it is.
- Factor in the space that you need to store your recycling- some schemes provide collection boxes but you will need to agree with school where these can be sited. If they can be put somewhere that parents

routinely walk past like the entrance hall this is great as it makes it easy for them to drop additional items in, but obviously health and safety with respect to potentially blocking entrances if there is restricted space needs to be considered.

School disco

Another traditional PTA fundraising method! Fun for the children, especially if they aren't held too often.

Tips:

- Decide if you are going to run it with a particular theme (if so have a look at Jubilee days in this A-Z) or as a general school disco.
- Work out what you want to provide as part of the disco- will you be providing a drink / snack for the children? (It's generally a good idea to make the children have a break halfway through so they don't get too hot or tired from all that dancing so they could have their drink and snack then).
- Once you know what you are providing as part of your entrance fee you can work out what to charge per child to make some money for the PTA.
- Work out the timings for the disco- when will it start? (too early and working parents won't be able to get their children there in time, too late and it will finish late which might be too tiring for little ones). Maybe if it is a large enough school you could run two discos- one for the younger children and one for the older children (who can stay up a bit later).
- Who is going to staff the event- just PTA members or will school staff help too? Some schools have a policy that if they are running a disco or similar event the staff need to stay to assist with the event- check this out with your school. Obviously if the school staff have to stay you need to make sure they are happy for the event to run. Take on board their thoughts on when an event might be

run- they won't want it in the middle of SATs week for example.

- Send out fliers to parents in advance, if you can get payment in advance this makes it easier to know how many children you are expecting (and need to buy snacks / drinks for) and one less thing to deal with on the night.
- Music:
    o Make sure you have a plan to make the disco music happen! Have you got a willing volunteer to be DJ? (PTA member or school staff).
    o If no DJ volunteer can you make a play list in advance?
    o Will you be letting children make requests for particular songs? If you have a DJ and suitable sound system they could do this on the night. If you are making up a playlist in advance, you could invite requests before the event (maybe ask on the flier that goes out to parents).
    o What do PTA members need to do to prepare on the day? Decorate the hall? Set up the sound system? Bring and set up the drinks and snacks? – make sure you know exactly what tasks need doing and when so you can set up a rota to fill with volunteers.
    o Do you want to make it an all inclusive event (i.e. the children have paid to go to the disco and a drink and snack is included) or do you want to set up other stalls such as nail or face painting that children can pay for? If you do then remember to tell parents so that they know to send their children with spending money.

Sponsored event for Parents

Some PTAs run sponsored sporting events with great success and raise large amounts of money from them. Some ideas on what to think about when looking at running this type of event are given below. The other way to raise money through sporting events for parents is for people to participate in an existing event in aid of the PTA. There are all sorts of events that people could enter- ironman type events, marathons, obstacle courses etc.

Tips:

<u>Running your own event</u>

- What sort of event would work well with your school population? Cycling? Walking? Swimming? Weight loss? Try and think about which would be most popular with your school population as you want the event to be well supported. If you are in an area where lots of people like walking or cycling they could be potential ideas.
- How will you run the event- will you just invite parents or will you open it up to the wider community? If you are opening it up to the wider community will you have a set number of places available? Will school parents be given the opportunity to register before the wider community? Is there a minimum number of entrants that you will need to make the event viable? If so will you state on your literature that you reserve the right to cancel the event and return payments if insufficient entries are received? If you are charging an entrance fee to secure places will this just be for the ability to participate in the event or will you include a branded event T shirt in the cost? (obviously this will increase the cost and what you need to charge but a package might make it more attractive to participants).
- Will parents be able to participate with their children or will it be just for parents (and if so can their children come and cheer them on)

- Will you give prizes for performance at the event? E.g. most lengths swum etc.
- Check your public liability insurance will cover you for whatever event you want to run. When you have decided what event to run see what information is available online for people wanting to run say a cycling event. Is there a local say cycling club who you could contact for advice? (and potential entrants if you decide to open the event up to the wider community).
- Think about the logistics of the event:
  - o Will you need people to be on hand to provide refreshments halfway round the route for example if you are running a sponsored cycle?
  - o Will you be charging an entrance fee and then asking people to raise sponsorship too? Or just relying on people raising money through sponsorship? What processes will you need to put in place to ensure the sponsorship money is collected by your deadline?
  - o Will you award special prizes to the people who raise the most money in sponsorship? If so what would the prizes be?
  - o Will you need to provide a first aider at the event?
  - o Will you be selling refreshments? If so what and where – at the start / finish line for something done on a route.

Entering an existing event

- If asking parents to enter existing events in aid of the school (in many ways this is the easier option in terms of organising), find out what events are coming up locally over the next few months.
- Put a flier out to parents asking for volunteers and give details of the events that are coming up to see if one event is particularly popular. Suggest on the flier that you want to put a team together and see how many volunteers for each event. Any parent that is willing to do

this sort of event in aid of the PTA should be supported as much as possible. If you have a few parents doing an event you could consider the following ideas to support them and get as much out of the event as possible:

- o Buy all participants matching branded T shirts with the PTA or school logo
- o Encourage other parents to come along and cheer them on at the event
- o Be willing to look after the participants' children at the event so they can concentrate on doing the event and not worrying about their children who can enjoy cheering them on
- o Be there and supplied to give the parents who are doing the event refreshments as needed
- o Offering a lift to the participating parents there and back (they might be able to drive themselves there but depending how tired they are afterwards they might appreciate not having to drive themselves home)
- o Promoting the forthcoming event on social media etc to encourage support and sponsorship.
- o Make sure any parent who does a sporting event in aid of the PTA is properly thanked, ideally both by the PTA and by the school to show how much their efforts are appreciated!

Sponsorship

Some PTAs are very good at getting sponsorship from local businesses. It is worth looking into whether this is an option for your PTA and if so the most suitable way. Sponsorship isn't always just about getting extra money in, if you can work a deal to save the PTA costs it would otherwise have to pay that can be just as worthwhile.

Tips:

- Think about how you could work with local businesses to

secure sponsorship. Some ideas are listed below:

- o Getting a local business to "sponsor" the school football or whatever team by providing the kit for all of the children to wear. In return the kit would display the logo of the business. This won't earn you money as they are providing the kit (or paying for it) but if the PTA had been asked to purchase the kit it means they no longer have to pay for it, leaving the money available to be used for something else.

- o Doing a business directory / producing a calendar where local businesses can pay to be included. Depending on how you work it, you can either charge all businesses to be in the calendar so that the payments more than cover the cost of producing it and it is given out to all parents for free (you make your money on what you charge the businesses to be included). Or you charge the parents for the calendars but raise a bit more money by allowing some businesses to be included for an agreed fee. If you are selling the calendar to parents you need to make it attractive to them to encourage sales- maybe by putting children's pictures in for each month.

- o What does the PTA spend a large amount of money on each year in running fundraising events? If you can identify these costs, see if you can think of businesses that might be able to sponsor them for example could you get a local printer to do all the PTA printing for a reduced price in return for displaying their logo on the work that they produce.

- o If you are running a big fair could you ask local businesses to sponsor individual stalls? Or could you use a business to give you a different way of fundraising such as getting a local car dealership to supply a car for the PTA to fill with balloons for a "guess how many balloons are in the car to win a prize" type competition? You could get them to supply the prize too so that way all you have do is run the stall (and blow the balloons up!). It would be an easyfundraiser to add to an existing event and something a bit different, and a cheap way for the car dealership to promote to potential new customers as they could be allowed to leave literature for people to pick up and their only real cost is the prize that they are providing for the competition.

o Working with businesses can also help if you want to have a high value raffle prize to increase entries. See if a local business will donate a prize in return for being able to say on the literature that goes out that it is supplied by them or if you can't find a business that will donate the prize outright, see if you can find one that will let you have it at cost price in return for being listed as a sponsor for the raffle / Christmas Fair etc.

o Consider offering a range of sponsorship packages to local businesses such as

- Inclusion in the information pack sent out to new parents for £20 (limited to five businesses) either in the form of fliers or putting their logos on the literature
- Placing of the business logo on the PTA newsletter that goes out to all parents at the school for the whole school year for £50 (limited to two businesses)
- Sponsorship of the stall of their choice at the Christmas Fair (as long as you are running one that year) from the list provided. This package would allow the business to have a banner on / above the stand and to be able to leave business cards or small fliers on the stall

itself for £75 (limited to two businesses).

- If you went with the examples suggested above and managed to sign businesses up to all the available sponsorship "slots" you would raise £350! Putting business logos on the newsletters would be easy as once you had updated your template for the year to include the logos you wouldn't have to change it again for the year, and as long as you made sure that the businesses who sponsored the stalls supplied you with the banners and fliers / business cards gave them to you in plenty of time that wouldn't be too much of an extra task for the amount of money it would bring in.

- You could also consider approaching companies with a "bespoke" sponsorship arrangement. If you were going to have a Black Tie Event / Ball you could offer companies the chance to sponsor it- you could discuss their requirements but perhaps having their logo on any tickets / menus / place cards etc and having a banner and branded balloons up in the entrance hall that guests would go through on their way to the ball in return for a few hundred pounds would be attractive to a company and would go a long way to reducing the costs to the PTA of putting such an event on.

- For all sponsorship arrangements with businesses, ensure that you are clear with them that payment is required in advance prior to the sponsorship arrangement commencing- it is easier this way than trying to chase a company for payment once they have had advertising in whatever form for a few months.

o Estate agents- some PTAs manage to raise quite a lot of money through sponsorship from estate agents. The most common way they do this is before a big event such as the Christmas Fair, the estate agents will put their boards up at parents' houses (obviously you need to persuade parents to allow this, and to check if they need to be the homeowner to be able to display a board) but instead of it saying "FOR SALE" or "SOLD", the space where that writing would be has details of the forthcoming event- date / time / venue and name of the event together with the PTA name so that it is clear that it is advertising the event in aid of your PTA. The estate agents will probably want a minimum number of houses that they can put boards up at and then they will pay the PTA per board they display. The going rate per board can be anything between £10-£40 per board displayed with estate agents usually displaying 25 boards and upwards. If you can find an estate agent who is interested in doing this, and enough parents who will allow the boards to be displayed it is well worth considering as if you had 25 boards at £20 each that would be £500 raised. The price the estate agent is willing to pay will depend on the area you are in, the proportion of homeowners in the area and how much competition there is locally for estate agents (if there are estate agent boards up all over the place, there is less incentive for them to want to pay to display more). The estate agents like this scheme because they get the opportunity to display boards (hence advertising) in areas that they may not normally work in, and people driving past will see the boards and may contact the estate agent about the property- although obviously the ones with your boards up aren't for sale, it gives the estate agent the chance to add a potential customer to their books for when they do get a property to market in that area. It also means that people living in the area see the board and may contact the estate agent when they come to look for an estate agent to sell their house if they want to move.

Sports Day Refreshments

A nice event for PTAs is to put on the refreshments at Sports Day. Whether this is done in order to make a profit or on a "break even" basis is up to you, but it is a nice opportunity for the PTA to be seen to be involved with school at an event where many parents will be present.

Tips:

- What refreshments do you want to offer? Tea / Coffee / Juice? Cake? Cream Teas?
- Do you want to run the event on a money making or a break even basis? You need to decide so that you know how much to charge (or you could offer Tea / Coffee / Juice at no charge as they are not expensive to provide if you decide not to run it as a money making event).
- If you are going to do cakes or cream teas, will you buy them in or ask for parental donations? Have you got anyone who would be willing to bake scones if they are provided with the ingredients?
- Make sure you have sufficient paper plates and cardboard cups to serve the refreshments- these are easier as no washing up afterwards; and probably safer if you are serving them outside.
- Have a contingency plan in place in case the weather is

bad and the event has to be postponed to another day! Tea / Coffee / Juice will be easy to store but what will you do with cakes / scones? Some cakes are freezable, available space permitting but it is good to have an idea of what could be done with large numbers of cakes etc. if the event does have to be postponed for any reason.

Summer Picnic

If you don't want to run a Summer Fair, but still want to have a Summer Event, you could consider running a Summer Picnic instead.

Tips:

- Where will you have it? School or somewhere else? It is an idea to have it somewhere that you can plan to be outside if the weather is kind, but have at least some indoor space available should it rain heavily.
- Have a contingency plan for rain! Fingers crossed you will have a lovely sunny day but if not what can you do to ensure that event can still run if the weather is bad. Do you have lots of parents with gazebos who might be willing to come and put them up to create a covered area outside? Having an indoor space will help enormously in the event of rain but if you can create a "gazebo village" that would allow at least some of the event to happen outside and continue the theme of the picnic.
- How will you structure the event? Will you sell sandwiches and other picnic food? Decide early on what food you want to provide and work out how much it is likely to cost so that you can work out what to charge people to come and make a profit. Will you sell alcohol? Having a cash bar can be a big profit maker but you will need to make sure that you comply with the licensing requirements where you are.
- Will you have entertainment such as music on for picnic goers? This can encourage them to stay longer and give

the event more of a party atmosphere. If you are putting music on will you be running a playlist / DJ or could you have a live band? Does anyone in the PTA have any contacts who might be able to find a band who would play for free / nominal fee in return for publicity. Depending on the size of your school and how many people you might expect to attend a summer picnic, consider if it is a good investment to pay a band to perform to ensure a successful event that people will want to come to again in the future. Having a band coming is another thing you can put on the publicity information you put out to make people want to come to your event.

- Will you have some stalls at the event? What would tie in with your summery theme? A strawberry and cream stall is summery and might appeal to people who fancy pudding after their picnic and who want a change from cakes if you decide to have a cake stall.
- Could you let the children bring a teddy bear so they could have a Teddy Bear's picnic?
- Unless there is good reason not to, have a raffle or tombola- these are such good ways to boost the funds raised by any event and people enjoy having the chance to win a prize either via tombola or raffle. Also consider having some fun stalls like hook a duck or similar to give people something else to do whilst they are at the event.

Supermarket Reward Vouchers

Many supermarkets run annual events where they give away vouchers for schools when people shop at their store. The more people spend, the more vouchers they are given. The schools then collect the vouchers from their parents and can combine them all to send off for free equipment (computers, gardening etc- depending on which scheme it is).

Tips:

- You need to collect an awful lot of vouchers to get some of the equipment on offer. That's not to say it isn't worthwhile doing these schemes, but it is better to think about them as an opportunity to get extra equipment as a bonus rather than setting your heart on a particular thing that the school needs, although if you do manage to get something that you would have otherwise had to buy this is great as you can then use the money you would have spent on something else.
- Keep reminding parents to collect the vouchers and send them in to school. You could set up a collection box in the hall (some schemes provide one to schools that register with the scheme) or ask parents to send their vouchers back in the weekly information bag.
- You will collect far more vouchers if you can get other people as well as just the parents at school to collect the vouchers.
  o Ask parents to ask their friends and family to give them any unwanted vouchers.
  o Keep posting on social media to remind people to collect them
  o Ask on local selling sites on social media if people have any unwanted vouchers. People like donating things to good causes, particularly if it hasn't cost them anything so if you can get people early on in the scheme on board then they may well collect the vouchers specifically for your school for the rest of the scheme
  o Ask people to ask their workmates for vouchers. If only one person in an office of ten people has school age children, and half the office shops at a supermarket that is running a voucher scheme, if that person asks everyone at work to collect vouchers for them they have a good chance of amassing significantly more

than if they just collected them on their own.

o If people have a work intranet for buying / selling, a wanted advert for vouchers can also get lots more vouchers. As they say every little helps but if every parent who worked in a large workplace did this, you would have the potential to collect many more vouchers than if you just asked parents to collect them.

Tombola

Tombolas are brilliant fundraisers! They are relatively easy to run, are popular (nearly everyone likes a go on the tombola) and can raise lots of money.

Tips:

- The basic jist of a Tombola is that you have lots of prizes on display. You use cloakroom tickets to put a number on each prize (usually easiest to put a number ending in 0 or 5). Then you discard the rest of the numbers off the strip you took your 0s and 5s from. The other set of numbers then gets folded individually and goes into the tombola. People then pay to pick the tickets out and if they get a ticket ending in a 0 or a 5 they know they have won a prize and then just need to match the number they have drawn to the one on the prize to find what it is.
- You will need a tombola drum to put the tickets in so that people can spin it and then pick tickets out to see if they have won. Amazingly these can be found on eBay if you don't already have one (but make sure you are getting one that you think is big enough if you do buy one off the internet)
- You can get your tombola prizes by buying them in, but you will raise far more money if you can get the prizes for free. Non uniform days where the children are asked to bring an item for the tombola are always good, as is just asking for donations. If you have a car boot sale or

jumble sale and anything brand new is left over that is another possible tombola prize (not clothes but books / ornaments / stationary etc- if you wouldn't mind winning it in a prize then it will be fine for the tombola)

- You can have a generic tombola where you just use any prizes you have and that will still make money. But for a bit of variety you can have a themed tombola:

  o Teddy Tombola- the children love these! You can ask people to donate unwanted teddies. If they aren't quite new you can always wash them if they look like they need it. You can sometimes pick up bargain brand new soft toys in charity shops if you need to boost numbers.

  o Rainbow Tombola- allocate a colour of the rainbow to each class / year group. Then ask each class / year to bring in an item that is suitable for a tombola prize in their allocated colour. You can then display the prizes in stripes of colour like a rainbow or mix them up.

  o Bottle tombola- tends to be a popular one. Again ask for donations but this time of new bottles. You will get all sorts from shampoo, tomato ketchup, and lots of alcohol.

  o Bottle tombola just with drinks- if you can collect enough bottles of alcohol you can just have a drinks tombola. Because of the value of the prizes (especially if you get a few bottles of spirits- you almost certainly will) then you can charge a bit more for this.

- Whichever sort of tombola you decide to have, remember you will have a lot of prizes if you have asked every child to donate a prize (unless you are a large school and then maybe you could ask each year group to donate a different thing for a non uniform day, but even one year group's worth of tombola prizes for a large school will be a lot of prizes to transport). You will need to factor this in when you are deciding how to get the prizes from school to wherever the tombola venue will be if it isn't at school.

- All the prizes will need a number attaching to them- don't leave this til the day of the event as it can be quite time consuming. If anyone is taking the prizes home to do this and has children, they might be able to help with this task. Remember to fold the tickets and put them in the tombola the night before too (or at least into a container to transfer into the tombola at the event) as folding 500 tickets takes time too.
- Blackjack lucky dip: another variant on the prize for a lucky dip theme- this time you have two decks of cards. Choose which cards will win a prize (Aces, Kings, Queens, Jacks). Stick these to the prizes and then let people choose a card from the other pack of cards. If they pick a winning card they win the prize it is attached to. Black Jack goes on the best prize. This works particularly well when the prizes are bottles of wine / spirits etc.

Treasure Hunt

Something a bit different and can be great fun! Maybe not the biggest fundraiser but people enjoy it and it is a nice extra thing to run from time to time. Children seem to love doing treasure hunts with their parents so it is a nice family activity that people can do at their convenience.

The basic principle is that people pay a fee to enter and are then given a list of questions with clues on how to find the locations they need to answer simple questions about. They then return their completed quiz sheets by a specified date and all correct sheets are placed into a draw to win prizes (and perhaps all correct entries get a small prize). Once you have written the questions and clues and distributed the sheets for sale you don't need to do anything except collect the completed sheets, check to see which are all correct and then do a draw of the correct ones to see who has won the prizes.

Tips:

- Don't make the clues so hard that people get fed up because they can't work them out and give up! You could make them get slightly harder with each question, but it is disappointing if you have paid to enter and then find you can't even work out where to go for the first question.
- Consider if you could get local businesses to sponsor a question each- if you make the location for their question their shop say, then that could bring in lots of extra footfall to their shop. You could either ask the business for a small cash sum or a nice item to use as a prize. If you can get a few businesses to donate a prize in return for sponsoring a question then you could make up a big hamper for first prize and maybe a couple of items for runner up prizes.
- You don't have to charge much for each entry as hopefully you will get most of your prizes donated and your only real cost will be the copying of the question sheets. £2 each or so is probably a reasonable sum.
- See if school will let you have a box for people to put their completed entries into so that it is easy for them to return them when they are finished, and easy for the PTA as they just have to go and get them from the box. Or people could send them back to school via their bulletin bags for school to collect and give to the PTA (or put in the collection box).

Uniform Sales

A great way to raise money but one that a surprisingly large number of PTAs don't seem to do. It can be done at next to no cost and is a great way for parents to buy school uniform at minimal outlay.

Tips:

- Plan this well in advance to give you time to tell parents you are collecting items of uniform in good condition. You will want to collect a reasonable amount of it before you have your first uniform sale so that you have a good selection of items in varying sizes to offer parents.

- Hopefully the parents at your school will be used to sending in unwanted clothes for your BagstoSchool collections. If they are, you just need to ask them to send the uniform items in separately. If not then this might be a good way to introduce them to the concept of sending in unwanted clothes to school, or introduce both collections at once making sure that parents know to separate uniform items from BagstoSchool items.

- Make sure parents know that uniform needs to be in reasonable condition i.e. not stained or with holes. PTAs that do uniform sales generally launder and iron all donated clothes which makes sense as it means they know for sure that the items have been freshly washed and are presented as well as possible which means they can be sold more easily. Once washed and ironed, make sure someone looks at all of the items to ensure that you are only selling good quality clothes that you would be happy for your children to wear. Anything that isn't up to scratch could be saved for BagstoSchool if storage is available (although check if your uniform has the school logo on it as they may not accept that).

- The uniform you have for sale shouldn't take up too much room- maybe one or two clothes rails. If it is much more than that it could become more time consuming in terms of setting it up at events, and also storing it in between events could become more difficult. Hopefully once you have started selling it you will find that you sell the majority of it and then can spend time collecting it again in time for the next one so you are never left with large quantities of uniform to store.

- Decide how you will price items. £1-£2 an item is probably fair- you will be getting the items for free so it is all pure profit (apart from having to buy a clothes rail if there isn't one you can borrow, and perhaps the odd tub of washing powder for whoever has the job of laundering the clothes). This means it is worth the PTA organising it (and for your volunteers to wash and iron everything so it is nice for people to buy) but can be a real benefit to parents who can save a lot of money on the costs of buying uniform.

- You could launch the uniform sales at the new parents' induction evening that most schools have in the summer term before their children start in September. Hopefully you already have a PTA member attending this event to give out new parent induction packs and to tell people about the PTA so it wouldn't be too onerous a task for them to sell the uniform whilst they are there.
- Have your clothes organised into item type (e.g. skirts, girls' trousers, jumpers, polo shirts, boys' trousers) on the rail and then in size order. You could have a label on each item so people can easily see the size and price. Although for a new parents' induction evening it would be tempting just to send the sizes you think would be useful for the children starting, if you have capacity you might send a few items for older children as some of the parents there may have older children already at the school.
- Hopefully selling the items will be straightforward- just ensure that the parents at the induction evening are told in advance that there will be a second hand uniform sale there so they can bring money with them, and make sure the person attending has a cash float with them.
- As well as being an extra fundraiser, running second hand uniform sales is a really good way of helping parents (and therefore their children) by saving them money on uniform costs. But it also helps the PTA as it increases awareness amongst parents of the PTA and how it can benefit the children at school which will hopefully encourage them to support other PTA events- either by volunteering to help run them or at least by going to them. Running a second hand uniform event at the new parents' induction evening will help make a positive impression to new parents of the PTA before they have even started at the school which can only be a

good thing.

- Once you've tested the uniform sales at the new parents' induction evening, you can hopefully then have it as a regular part of other events such as PTA Coffee mornings, Christmas Fair, Summer Fair

Voucher sales

This is where PTAs buy vouchers from retailers to sell to parents to use to do their shopping. The money is raised because the school gets a discount for bulk buying vouchers which are then sold at facevalue. The trick is to get parents to sign up to a monthly standing order so that they are buying vouchers (or gift cards depending on the retailer) every month so the PTA is getting a regular income and isn't having to take payments for the orders every month, it just has to distribute the vouchers.

Tips:

- Research the different retailers that have a voucher scheme. They are often more set up for business users. There are also special voucher companies that will sell vouchers to all sorts of shops that give varying discounts for bulk buying. Anecdotally, it seems that it is becoming harder to join voucher schemes directly with retailers so if you find this is the case, it may be worth researching the companies that deal in vouchers from all retailers.
- If you can get a family to commit to buying £100 vouchers a month to do their regular shop and the retailer gives you a 2.5% discount for bulk buying, that would raise £2.50 a month. Not a huge amount on its own but if you get 10 families all signing up that is £25 a month- £300 a year which is more worthwhile. Some retailers allow the vouchers to be used online- they all have slightly different schemes (and the discounts given for bulk buying vary) so you need to research the different retailers, voucher companies and discounts

given on the different retailers' vouchers.

- You need to buy a certain amount of vouchers to qualify for the bulk buying discount. If you are a smaller school you may struggle to get enough orders to do this, but some schools get round this by teaming up with other schools in the area. This allows them to combine their orders so between them they qualify for the discount and can all make a profit on the orders from their parents.
- If you are interested in this method of fundraising, you will probably need a named volunteer to be in charge of running the scheme for your school (taking orders, talking to parents who are interested in joining the scheme, making sure standing order instructions from new parents are registered with the bank, giving the vouchers out to parents each month).
- Many schools run this scheme from September – July so that they are not required to do anything with it in August, over the summer holidays.
- As the discount varies between retailer you need to research the retailers that offer the scheme to new entrants. As you need to order a certain amount (also varies between retailers) to qualify for the discount you should also research which retailers your parents use most as they would be retailers you are likely to get the most voucher orders for and therefore qualify for the discount. So rather than signing up to lots of schemes, maybe initially look at signing up for the retailer most used by parents as this will increase the chance of parents signing up to order vouchers and you qualifying for the bulkbuy discounts. The alternative to just signing up with one retailer initially is to look at the specialist voucher companies who may allow you to mix and match vouchers from different retailers.
- Setting up and running this scheme is time consuming, but it is worth looking into- some schools are raising hundreds of pounds a year in this way. If you have to team up with other schools locally in order to make it viable in terms of securing enough orders to qualify for the discount (i.e. profit) this might seem daunting initially

but still worth looking at as all PTAs are keen to find new ways of raising money so may be receptive to the idea. If you can form a partnership arrangement with other PTAs to run the scheme it also gives the additional bonus that you have built working relationships with other PTAs which could be useful for other things such as if you ever wanted to run a joint event with other PTAs.

Zumba!

Zumba is proving a popular activity – both for people who like dancing and for its fitness benefits. It has potential to be used as a fun fundraiser!

Tips:

- Think about how you would run the event- would it be a sponsored Zumbathon, or a Zumba class run in conjunction with the PTA? The Zumbathon might attract more publicity and therefore entrants and sponsorship.
- You would need to find a Zumba instructer who would be willing to help with the event. Zumba is increasingly popular so there should be a few instructers around. Hopefully they would be keen to be involved because of the publicity they might be able to get, and therefore the potential to get new customers.
- Send out information in advance including sponsorship details so that people have as much time as possible to get sponsored for the event, but make sure that people have to register to join the event so that you know how many people you are likely to get (you could make it clear that places are limited to try and encourage people to submit their registrations in time).
- Consider whether you will provide refreshments at the event and how you will manage spectators- will there be room for anyone to come and watch or will space be limited?
- Promote the event on social media so that you can encourage sponsorship for the participants.

- If you don't want to do a Zumba-thon but you think you may have a group of parents who would like to learn how to do Zumba, you could see if any instructers would be willing to come and teach them if you provide the class. You could try and get a discount from the Zumba instructer for teaching the class (in return for providing them with a new class of people) and add a small mark up to the cost of joining the class in order to make a profit. Maybe once your Zumba class has learned how to do it, they might then be able to do a sponsored Zumbathon!

A-Z of smaller fundraising ideas for use at larger events in combination

(brief explanation provided for those that do not have their own section in main A-Z)

100 Square

Very simple but effective. Make a large square diagram with 100 smaller squares, numbered 1-100. Have the squares large enough to put contact name and number in. Sell the squares at £1 each. Winning number is picked at random (you can use a random number generator app / website) and the winner gets £25 (and the PTA gets £75). People like the chance of winning £25 for the sake of spending £1!

Book stall

Ask children to donate an as new unwanted book each (again another Non Uniform day possibility). Collect the books up and sell them on a book stand at bargain prices but as they were donated you will make a profit. Keep any that don't sell for the next time if you have the storage available.

Brantub / Lucky Dip

Have a big container like a garden truckle and fill it with sawdust or similar. Have lots of small prizes (you can get small cheap prizes on ebay) in there. Children pay a certain amount to get their dip in the Bran Tub / Lucky Dip and as long as you are charging more than it cost you per toy to buy the prizes you will make a profit.

Cake stall

See Cake Stall section in main A-Z

Candy Floss / Popcorn

You can get a candy floss maker, sugar and sticks quite cheaply (less than £30-£40 with enough to start you off) from Amazon. Children love candy floss so if you have a candyfloss stall you should be able to recoup the initial outlay within one event or two (depending on what you charge) and then after that this is a profitable and popular addition to your event as you would just have to cover the cost of the sugar and sticks and could probably charge £1 for each candyfloss. You would need power for your candy floss machine though.

Popcorn works on a similar principle- once you have bought your popcorn maker and recouped the purchase cost, this is another high profit seller as popcorn is cheap to buy.

Carols

See Carol Section in main A-Z

Crafting Stall

If you are just running one crafting stall as part of a larger event then you need to decide what activity to run.

Something that is relatively simple that large elements of can be prepared in advance is probably sensible (so you're not trying to cut bits out whilst also helping numerous children do the activity). Also if it is something that might need to sit and dry for a while, will you have space available to put all the drying things the children have made? If not you may need to consider another activity.

Grotto

If you can have a Santa's Grotto at your Christmas Fair, that will be popular with children and set off the Christmassy atmosphere of the event perfectly. You will need a Santa! You will also need a small room to decorate as the grotto with tinsel / wrapping paper/ fake Christmas tree etc. Have Santa's presents ready for him (Santa might want a couple of sacks so he knows one is full of presents for younger children, the other for older children) so the children can go in and see him to get their present. Santa will need an elf or two for assistance. Charge enough that you make a profit on the present but not so much that children aren't able to go to see Santa because it is too expensive.

Guess weight of the cake

If you get a nice cake donated, or can persuade someone to make one, you can do a guess the weight of the cake competition. Weigh the cake in advance so you know the weight. Have a form where people can write their guesses down along with their contact details for 50p-£1 a go. Then at the end of the event the person closest to the correct answer wins the cake. Whoever is running this needs to make sure each guess put down is different so you don't risk having more than one correct answer. This can be run on another stall like the cake stall so is a relatively easy way to raise a bit more money and works particularly well for a heavy or large cake.

Hook a duck

For this you need some plastic ducks that will float, an inflatable paddling pool filled with water for the ducks to go into and some hooks on sticks. It works better if the ducks each have a wire loop on them so they are easy to catch with the hook, but if not as long as they can be caught by hooking round their necks to get them out will work. Have some inexpensive prizes (you can buy "party bag" type toys in bulk off eBay, or use anything else that you have e.g. left over prizes from another event that would be suitable for children). People get to "hook a duck" for 50p a go or three for £1 say and get a prize for each duck they catch. As long as your prizes are costing you less each than what you are charging to hook a duck this will make a profit once you have covered the cost of the equipment, but this is inexpensive.

Plant Stall

Plants can do well at a Fair. Christmassy plants at a Christmas Fair, bedding plants / flowering bulbs at an Easter or Summer Fair. Either get them from your local garden centre and see if you can have them on sale or return and if they will give you a discount or see if any local discount shops or DIY stores are selling them cheaply enough for you to buy them to sell on at a profit.

Raffle

See the Raffle (and Christmas Raffle) sections in the main A-Z

Refreshments

If you can sell refreshments at any event this is likely to boost the amount you raise. Tea and coffee aren't too expensive to buy in terms of cost per cup so there is room to make a decent mark up on the drinks that you sell. You can get soft drinks quite cheaply too if you shop around (if you have a Homebargains or similar locally that is worth checking out as they do single soft drinks cans very cheaply) which you can add a mark up to without making them too expensive. Soup is a good addition to any event where people might want it (so maybe not at a Summer Fair if it is hot)- you can make a lovely soup quite cheaply and if you do soup and a roll, you can buy rolls in bulk quite cheaply from supermarkets so this can also make a reasonable profit.

If you are selling refreshments and you get some nice cakes or scones donated to the cake stall, consider if you would raise more money from them by selling them in slices / as cream teas from the refreshments table rather than for people to take home.

Table top sale

If you are having an event and think you might have space for extra stalls, consider having a table top sale. Charge each stall holder £5-£10 a table for them to bring unwanted second hand items to sell. People like the chance to get a bargain so these stalls tend to do well and it is a helpful way to fill up your hall if you are a few stalls short. If you do end up having a few table top sale stalls you could group them together so you have a mini Table Top sale area

Toy stall

You could ask for donations of any unwanted / outgrown

nearly new toys before an event and then run a second hand toy stall. Any Fair you run is likely to have lots of children attending so a toy stall should do well. Remember you need to make sure the toys are in good condition and safe though so consider specifying only new / nearly new toys- you might get less but the quality will be higher so you could charge more.

Animals- Pony Rides / Reindeer

Children like animals so they can be a popular addition to any event. But you need to be careful adding animals- if you want to do pony rides for example you need to make sure you are covered by your public liability insurance, many policies may not cover this automatically. You may be required to hire someone to bring a pony for rides rather than letting a parent bring their pony along to get insurance cover. If a parent volunteers to bring their pony and says they are insured, you would need to check if their insurance covered them for charging for rides. You would also need to ensure that the all children riding wore a riding hat and that the hat complied with the current safety requirements for hats. Ponies are lovely, and children adore pony rides but accidents can happen so it is really important to make sure that you are happy this is as safe as possible and that you are fully insured to try and minimise against accidents and insured if something does happen. Some areas might have stables set up to bring ponies (or donkeys) along for events with their own insurance and this can be worth looking into.

Some PTAs hire reindeer to be there at their Christmas Fairs! This certainly adds to the spectacle of the event, but again you would need to ensure all insurance was in place, and clarify where the reindeer would be (would the reindeer people provide a corral for them or would you need to) and would children be able to pat them or would they just be to look at?

Animals are nice to have at Fairs but do make sure you have researched everything carefully before you arrange to bring them to an event.

Enterprise stalls for the Children

If school can be persuaded to run an enterprise project with the children (they make things and then sell them to teach them how to make money from a business idea) then having enterprise stalls at the Fair is a great boost to fundraising. This is because if children are asked to be at the event to run their own enterprise stalls, they are more likely to come and if they come they will bring family members who will hopefully spend money at the Fair. You could run a competition to give the child who makes the most money from their stall a prize. The children can choose to run their enterprise stalls in aid of a charity as another incentive for them to come to the event, you don't make money from their stalls directly it is the people that they bring with them that spend money at other things at the Fair that boost your fundraising so it doesn't matter if the enterprise stalls are running in aid of another charity.

Photographs

If you have a parent who is a good photographer (professional or gifted amateur) who is willing, you could add a photographic element to your fair. For example you could charge a fee for children to see Santa which would include a photograph of them with Santa. You would need a system to either print the photos off there and then (you can get wallets or clear plastic bags to put the photographs in) to give to parents, or be able to know for sure which photograph should be sent to the right parents after the event. The other option is to see if there is a professional photographer who would like to do photoshoots with children at the Fair in return for a percentage of their takings on the day. This would need some more managing as you would have to have timeslots to prebook but it is a nice extra draw for a Fair if you do have a photographer who would like to do this.

Guess the teacher

Simple but fun! Ask all the teachers to bring in a photo of them as a baby or young child. Put them in clear plastic or similar to protect them and display on a board, with each photograph having a number. Then have a numbered sheet so that people can guess for each photograph which teacher they think it is. You could charge 50p-£1 to enter and the person who gets the most right wins a prize (or a prize for all correct answers). Make sure you look after the photos well and know who they all are so you can return them to the right teachers afterwards!

11 BIG EVENTS

Many of the PTAs I researched who were raising higher amounts of money had a strategy where they had a few key events throughout the year which were their main fundraisers. These ranged from Christmas Fairs to Annual Balls and Promise Auctions. To varying degrees they also did other, smaller events throughout the year but the main focus of their fundraising activities were a small number of large, high earning events.

The return can be high on a Big Event so it is definitely worth considering running one, but they do require an extra level of organisation to be successful.

Tips:

- Plan well in advance. Months if necessary! Better to be really far ahead of yourselves and be able to just give brief updates than to be the other way and panicking or worse still find that you have left it too late and cannot run the event after all, say because the venue you wanted is now booked up.
- When you have decided what event you want to run, consider having a special meeting just to plan that event. You can set up a subcommittee of particular PTA members who have agreed to run the event if this is easier than having a full PTA meeting, but remember to check your Constitution- some may specify that any Sub-Committee has at least one PTA Committee member or even the Chair or Secretary or Treasurer on it.

- Draw up a list of things that need to be looked at and planned for your big event. These could include (but not be limited to):
  - Date: Is there a preferred date? Are there any dates we need to avoid?
  - Venue: Do we know which one we want? If not do we have a list to choose from? Do we need to view them and get quotes? When do we need to book by? Do we need to pay a deposit and if so by when? When do we have to pay the balance?

    If we do know which venue we want, is it available on the date we need and have we booked it yet?
  - Refreshments / food : What refreshments are needed? Who will provide them? If caterers do we need to get quotes and choose a caterer? How much will it cost per person? Do we need to pay a deposit and if so by when? When do we have to pay the balance? When do we have to choose the menu?

    If not using a caterer- what refreshments do we want to provide? Are we doing this on a break even or profit making basis? How much will it cost to provide the refreshments per serving and are these to be factored into the overall cost of each ticket (if refreshments / food are included in the ticket price) or if not how much do we need to sell each thing for to either break even or make a profit?

    Are we going to sell alcohol at the event? If so who will make sure that the event complies with Licensing requirements. Where will the alcohol be bought from? Who will organise that? Do we need glasses or are they provided with the venue? If we need glasses can we rent some? Someone will need to organise that and then arrange for their collection and then return after the event. When do they need booking by?

o Does the venue need decorating? If so how? Who will do it? When can we get into the venue before the event to decorate it? Can it be cleared the day after the event or does everything need to be removed immediately afterwards? Who will do it?

o Are we providing any other things at the event. Such as band? If so do we have one? How much will it cost? If we don't have one, what is our budget? How do we choose one? Again, is a deposit payable and by when? When do we have to pay the balance?

o Have we identified all costs that we will incur to run the event so that we can set the ticket price to make a profit? (you really don't want to go to all the work of running an event to make a profit and then find you don't because you didn't add up the costs correctly).

o Are we running any other projects within this event? E.g.

  ▪ Tombola- who will run it? How will we get the prizes? If non uniform day- when will that be held? When will we put out the notification? Who will collect up the prizes, put the numbers on, set up the tombola at the event? The treasurer will need to provide a float.

- Raffle- again who will run it? Can we try and get any big prizes donated? If so, do we need to write out to businesses to ask for donations / sponsorship? Who will do that? Will we use cloakroom tickets on the night or run a bigger raffle with printed tickets that we will also try and sell in advance? If so, who will organise for the tickets to be printed and sent out to parents in advance. Who will make sure we record any information needed for submission afterwards to comply with the Gambling Licence?

  - Any PTA stalls- who will be running them? Are any donations needed for them (e.g. cake stall). How will we notify parents that we need donations and who will organise collection of them and transportation to the event?

- If we are inviting external (non PTA) stall holders to the event- how much will we charge? What sort of booking system are we going to have and who will run it? How will we advertise that we have stalls available for our event? Will we make sure that we do not have duplication of stalls and that we do not book too many stalls?

- Have we confirmed that our public liability covers us for everything we want to do at this event? If not who will?

- How are we going to advertise this event to either sell all of the tickets or to get as many people as possible coming to the event on the day.

- You can see that there are an awful lot of things to think about and organise for a big event! One approach that works well is to put particular people in charge of particular elements of the event- it will be too big for any one person to manage on their own. So you could have person in charge of running refreshments, one person doing the raffle etc. They may need extra support with some elements but if every task has been delegated to a named person, this will break it down into a more manageable workload for each person.
- Have regular PTA (or sub committee) meetings to monitor progress and identify work that is still to do. If you have any parents who are particularly good at project management, see if you can rope them in to help. Make it clear you aren't necessarily wanting them to run the cake stall, but you would appreciate their project management skills to assist in organising to event as a whole.
- Communication is key- make sure everyone is kept in the loop and no-one who needs to know a key piece of information is left out. Make sure everyone knows who is in charge of which element of the event, and who is in charge overall.
- Identify deadlines that need to be met in relation to the project once you know them. E.g. when all the various things that have to be booked (venue, band, caterer, glasses....) have to be booked by and what payments have to be made and when. Also the dates and deadlines in relation to related tasks like the Non Uniform day you will need to run to supply the prizes for the tombola. Try and record all required actions and deadlines in an overall plan with who is responsible for each marked down too. This will help keep track of overall progress and tasks that still need action.

When you are in the final week or so before the event, it can be useful to do an action plan of things that will need attention in the run up to the event and the event itself. Distribute it to all of your volunteers so everyone knows what is still to do, and who should be doing it to save peoples' time asking different people who is doing what. Whoever is in overall control of the event can then ensure that the tasks are completed and tick them off so that everything is done in time.

An example action sheet is below. This is one that was actually used in an event. It is from a couple of weeks before the Fair that it was for, but shows how breaking everything down into specific tasks and showing the people responsible for them was really helpful as everyone knew what they were meant to be doing. It was then updated a few days before the event to show what still needed to be done (and to add the names of the volunteers we had managed to get!)

Advent Fair and Table top Sale info / action sheet
Venue and timings: Village Hall. 10-1 (booked from 9-2 to allow for set up and clear away)
Sandra / Helen: Village Hall lady says that it will fit 18x 6ft tables and 8 x
4 ft tables. She suggests having the larger tables around the edges for stalls and then using the 4ft tables for teas coffees etc. She suggested having the t/c tables in front of the stage, alternatively I have seen it done to the left of the hall by the kitchen which also worked well. If you still want to view she can do this Sat am early or an evening next week (not Weds / Thurs). Her number is 692731 if you do want to view, might make sense if you contact her direct to arrange when. If you don't want to please let me know so I can tell her.
Table info:

Table	Details	Confirmed/ Action required
Cake Stall	PTA	Need volunteers
Reindeer food / used books	PTA	Need volunteer
Tombola	PTA	Need volunteers
Raffle tickets / guess weight of cake	PTA	Need volunteers Need to ask Catherine if she will do this year Need raffle prizes(Mrs K said staff doing a hamper too) Need raffle tickets- Sophie getting today
Secret String /bricabrac	PTA/ Sandra C	Sandra C
Teas/ coffees/ bacon rolls / soup	PTA	Elisabeth asking (parents who run butchers) re bacon Need to get buns – ASDA order? Investigate soup- Mrs Tetley volunteered to help serve. Did Orla volunteer to make the soup?
Chutneys / Jams / breads	Mrs Fielding	Booking form sent
Bricabrac	Stacey Smith	Booking form sent
Local Charity stall	Local Charity	Booking form sent

	stall	
Sewn decorationsetc	Juliet	Booking form sent
Amy Knight	Pictures	Booking form sent
Laura Robbins	Avon / Pictures	Booking form sent
Stacey Shepherd	Usborne books	Booking form sent
Beverley	Scarves andbricabrac	Waiting for confirmation she still wants table
Anita Findlay	Waiting to find out	Has expressed interest in table, waiting to find out what she does- do we want more tables or are we happy with what we have?
Craft table	PTA	Need tree to hang baubles on Need volunteers

Flier- Laura Robbins doing. Need asap- to go out in this weeks bag and to put round village etc. Can we put signs up on the roads around the village eg like they do for car boot sales etc? Sent Laura last years flier for info. Have asked Mrs Fielding if we can laminate some for putting outside and also if we can have some in A3. Have emailed Laura with info today.

Raffle- Sophie getting tickets today. Laura and Elisabeth to sort out putting into bags (talk to Mrs Fielding / Anne for how to do it)

Letters out in bag:

- Tombola / raffle prize request – Helen doing
- Cake stall donations – Helen done flier. Sandra C sorting out paper plates
- Volunteer request- Helen doing

Remember, once the event is over and the amount that was raised is known- tell people! Hopefully it is a lot of money and everyone will be really pleased. Lots of people will have been involved with the event- in organising it, volunteering on the day, the parents that donated prizes for their children to have Non Uniform Day, the school etc.- they will all want to know how much was raised! Tell people whilst it is still fresh in their minds and they will remember what a success it all was, and think how worthwhile it was and be more willing to be involved next time! If you don't tell anyone until the next meeting, the moment will have been lost and it will be a lost opportunity in terms of engaging with parents and sharing the success of the PTA and what it can achieve which can help you get more people on board for the future. This goes for any fundraising event that the PTA does, but is especially important for big events as you will have had so many people involved, and hopefully the sum raised will be worth announcing!

12 SCHOOL FAIRS

This is just a short section about School Fairs specifically. The previous chapter gives information about how to plan for a big event, much of which will apply to Fairs, but this section gives some additional tips that are more relevant to Fairs

Tips:

- When are we having the Fair and will it have a theme? The two questions tend to go together for School Fairs- It is an important question as it will guide you with respect to:
    - o Venue: If your Fair is winter you will probably want an indoor venue. If it is Spring or Summer then you may decide to take a chance and try an outdoor venue
    - o Theme: If you are having a Fair in winter the chances are you will be doing a Christmas Fair; in Spring you may be doing an Easter Fair etc.

- Once you know your venue and theme you can start to plan your event. What stalls / activities will you have at your Fair? The Fundraising ideas chapter has lots of suggestions for large and small stalls and activities but this is worth considering carefully. You want to have a nice mix of stalls and activities- duplication with too many similar stalls / activities will mean the Fair is less successful than a Fair with a broad variety of stalls / activities to increase the chances of appealing to more people there (and therefore them spending more money).

- Try to think of categories of stall / activity you want to have at the Fair and then you can identify which ones you want to run.

  -For a Christmas Fair you could choose to have:
  - o Santa's Grotto
  - o Cake Stall
  - o Christmas Raffle
  - o Nearly new Toy Stall
  - o Refreshments : Tea / Coffee / Soup and a Roll
  - o Facepainting
  - o Bran Tub

  -For a Summer Fair you could choose to have:
  - o Cake Stall
  - o Tombola
  - o Book Stall
  - o Refreshments: Tea / Coffee / Soft Drinks / Icecream
  - o Candy floss
  - o Nail painting
  - o Hook a duck

You will probably want more stalls / activities than are listed above. The examples are intended to demonstrate how you should try to vary the different stalls that you have at the different events- both to adapt them to the event that you are having, and to keep them "fresh". If you have exactly the same stalls at every event that you do, people will get bored and be less keen to come. If you vary them so it is something different each time people will hopefully maintain their interest and be keen to come to your events. Be careful to replace items of a certain fundraising potential with another of similar fundraising potential- such as have a

Christmas Raffle but then for a Summer Fair you could have a Tombola. Both of these can raise large amounts of money. Be aware of the likely amount that each of your fundraising ideas is likely to have and take this into consideration when you are deciding which to put on- if you are running an event to make money you need to make sure you have a few "high earning" elements included.

Don't forget, you will need volunteers to help with all the stalls on the day as well as hopefully the preparation and any clear up work afterwards. Make sure everyone knows you need volunteers, and if you are struggling approach people in person as they are more likely to say yes to requests for help! It is so important at the event to look after your volunteers- if you can have one person who will go round and relieve the volunteers behind the stalls so they get the chance for a wander around the event rather than being stuck behind the stall for the whole time they will feel much more appreciated. Bringing them all a cup of tea whilst they are working on the stall also shows that they are valued. And make sure that they are all thanked for their help afterwards.

Anne Dunn

13 TIPS FOR TREASURERS

This section is designed to help the Treasurer of your PTA, but hopefully will be interesting reading for all readers of this book. The Treasurer role is demanding as they have to be involved in every event by way of providing floats / counting money / paying expenses / banking and accounting for all the money. Although they can delegate responsibility to some degree if they cannot physically attend an event, they are still responsible overall for the money and PTA annual accounts which then have to be audited. This chapter gives tips and suggestions for methods that I found helped me when I was PTA Treasurer.

- Keep records of everything! You may remember, but in a years time when you have to do the yearly accounts you will be glad that you wrote it down because by then the chances are you may not remember the details of what you needed to remember.
- I found it very helpful to have an A4 cash book where I wrote everything down by hand. This meant it was to hand by my side as I was working on Treasurer tasks, rather than having to write things down and then put on the computer later- with young children and a job the chances are "later" would be much later. If you have everything written down as you are doing it, this makes it a much easier task to sort the computing out when you get the time (!).
- In my book, I kept the following as separate pages:
    o Money put into bank: The date, amount put in and what the money was from was recorded- a line for each. If I banked money from more than one event I would record them separately (this helps when you come to do your end of year accounts as you can see

exactly what money was banked for each event and how much money each event made so you can produce a breakdown of fundraising over the year by event which is useful for comparison purposes and deciding what events to do in following years).

- o Cheques written: The date, the cheque number, the amount, who to and what for (e.g. 1/6/13- 000357- £17.63- Sandra Cook-Ingredients to bake cakes for cake stall). This lets you have a record of what you have spent putting on individual events in one place (you will also record this under the section for each event) and will let you see if any cheques are still to be cashed and if so who needs chasing to do it.

- o Each Event: Each event had its own page. In here I wrote the float the event had, any money spent putting the event on, and the amount of money taken after the event. I also used to write the amount banked broken down into denominations / cheques to match the bank pay in slip. Remember to remove the amount you put in as float as well as the expenses you paid out before working out the total you raised. If each event has its own page it is much easier to go back and record an additional transaction such as if someone puts a receipt in for an expense they incurred a couple of weeks after the event. Also, if possible try and make a separate cheque payment for each set of expenses ie. If someone claims for £25 made up of £10 on cake stall ingredients and then £15 on raffle tickets for a separate raffle you should do two cheques (£10 + £15) so that it is clearer for you to track spending for each event when you come to do your accounts, and you can see more clearly exactly what each event raised. Make sure you record each cheque separately under your overall cheques paid out page as well as under the payments made on the specific page for each event.

o For events with multiple fundraising elements e.g. a Fair with different stalls- make sure these are all recorded separately so you can see how much each stall raised. You can total it all afterwards and pay in one large amount of money from the whole Fair but make sure you know how much each stall etc. from a large event made.

o Overall total of how much money the PTA has raised (raised as in the profit you have made, not the amount of income you have received) as the year goes on. You might need to amend this if you get an extra expenses claim a few weeks after an event, but this is a really useful thing to have. It means that if anyone asks you how much the PTA has raised this year, you can tell them without having to work it out. It also means it is easy for you to include this in your Treasurers report at PTA meetings. You can also then easily issue an end of term announcement to say how much money has been raised so far that school year and that term which is a great thing to do as it is nearly always more than people think (all the various totals from the different events do add up) so it is a great motivator for all the PTA volunteers, and hopefully an encouragement for other people to become involved with their PTA.

- Always pay expenses via cheque – this gives you a better record rather than in cash back to someone at the event with the cash that you have just taken at the event. This is just better financial record keeping and makes sure everything is recorded for future years. It also protects you as Treasurer as you can demonstrate that you always put everything through the books. If you are introducing this rule, just make sure people know in advance and explain why and they will get used to it.
- For events that parents have to pay for in advance- write down the payments you have received and are banking e.g. if people are paying £5 a child you can total all the cash you have received; for cheques you should record each individual cheque amount as well as the total. Keep a list of who has paid too! This will help you if you ever have a cheque bounce (it happens) as you will find it easier to work out which event the cheque was for from the amount the cheque was for and when it was paid in (sometimes you end up having to get cheques in from people for various different events at the same time).
- Bank everything separately- even if you are having to go to bank money from more than one event, ensure that each event has its own paying in slip filled in. This way when you come to do the accounts it is far easier as you will be able to match the amount you banked for each event with the amounts put in as shown on the bank statements.

- Have a specific PTA Treasurer drawer / bag / storage area in your house! In an ideal world you would be able to file everything as you receive it. In real life with children / jobs / other commitments you may find that you can't always do this straightaway. If you have your PTA Treasurer drawer or whatever make it a rule that even if you can't deal with any piece of paper that you receive relating to the role (you will get lots of pieces of paper) you will ALWAYS put them straight into your Treasurer drawer. This means that when you do sit down to do your Treasurer work you don't then have to waste time looking for the bits of paper because they will all be in your Treasurer drawer. This might sound silly, but in four years of being Treasurer I found this was probably the most important thing to do as there is nothing more frustrating than wasting time you don't have trying to find that one vital bit of paper!

- Keep all the bank statements! As above, if you can't put them in a folder straightaway, at least put them in your Treasurer drawer so that they are there ready to be filed when you are ready to do the filing. You will need to present your folder of bank statements together with your yearly accounts at some point to be audited so need to have them to hand. If you do lose a statement don't panic, you can usually get the bank to print you off another copy but this means a trip to the bank which will take more time (after you have already wasted time looking for the elusive bank statement before deciding you can't find it and have to get another printed off). So put the bank statements in your Treasurer drawer as soon as they arrive.

- You should open your bank statements monthly and check the transactions against what you have paid in and what payments you think should have gone out. You also will need to record any payments that come out automatically (rather than by cheque) such as if you are a PTA-UK member, they tend to take the money by annual direct debit. You may also have payments that go into your bank automatically such the quarterly payment from easyfundraising. You will need all your bank statements there for when you come to do your annual accounts to make sure that every transaction is recorded in your accounts.

- Every payment you make should have a receipt. This includes claims for expenses from other PTA members- when you start as Treasurer (or as soon as you read this book if later) you really need to tell everyone that from now on if they want to claim any expenses they must provide a receipt. You need these to justify the expenses payments you make, and to keep in your folder along with the bank statements and accounts. Put it on the agenda for the next PTA meeting so that you can inform the meeting and they can approve the new rule and that way it is in the minutes too for future record.

- If you have just started as Treasurer, find out what information you are expected to report at the regular PTA meetings. Some just require the current bank balance of the PTA bank account(s). Others will want a more detailed breakdown of all payments made and money banked since the last meeting together with an update of the total amount of money raised so far that year. If you know in advance what information you will need to bring to each meeting you will be able to set up your system so that this information is easily to hand. Hopefully you will have had a good induction and handover when taking over the Treasurer role so that you already know what is required, but if not find out as you don't want to go to your first meeting and be expected to give information that you don't have because nobody told you that you needed to present it and they assumed that you had been told.

- Floats: As Treasurer you will need to provide a float for any fundraising activities that involve taking payments. This is relatively straightforward for a single activity but can get more complicated if it is a large event like a Fair where you have lots of stalls. Some tips for doing floats are below:

  o Know how much float you have provided. You need to know this so that you can deduct it when working out how much money the stall has raised.

  o Floats can be put in a variety of containers- the container you choose should be influenced by what you have available and also how much money you are expecting the event to take. For example if it is just a small stall say nail painting, you could probably get away with a smallish float in a margarine or takeaway tub. But for a large or popular stall that is going to take large amounts of money such as a cake stall or tombola you want a larger, sturdier container such as a metal biscuit tin. All your float containers need lids. It is a good idea to make a label to stick on your float tub saying what the float is for (e.g. cake stall), how much the float is (e.g. £10) and who is in charge of the stall. This means when you get it back after the event you know how much the float was, the stall it was from and who you need to speak to if there were any discrepancies. Put the label on the container itself rather than the lid to prevent any accidental mix ups with the wrong lid ending up on the wrong container. It can be an idea to send multiple floats in all different containers to try to prevent this happening but putting the label on the container will reduce the chances of a mix up.

o For an event with multiple stalls where you have to provide lots of floats, it is a good idea to have a list of all the stalls and floats. That way you know which float to give to which stall because each float container is labelled (remember you may be giving different float amounts in different sized tubs depending on how much money you think each stall will take so you do need to make sure the right float goes to each stall). This also means at the end of the event you can tick off on your list when you get each float back to make sure that you have got them all back.

o Good practice says that money should really be counted by two people present together. This guards against any misunderstandings or accusations about any discrepancies with the money. If you can do this then you should, but if you are a small PTA this isn't always possible. It is up to your own PTA to decide if it wants to make this a requirement of managing money that it makes at events. You do want to try and get the money counted and banked as quickly as possible after the event- so that you can tell people how much it raised and so that the money isn't lying around in the event of a burglary (unfortunately it can happen) so the PTA would need to take this into account when deciding if it prefers to insist that money is counted by two people (which might not be possible immediately after the event) or if it prefers to get the money processed and banked as soon as possible to minimise the risk of theft by burglary. Each PTA will have its own answer on this but it is a good idea to get clarification if you are just starting in the role.

14 SAMPLE TEMPLATES

This section gives sample documents for various purposes. These are intended to give ideas for wording and layout to help PTA members design their documents for their use. Obviously you will need to insert your own PTA and School details such as name / address / registered Charity numbers as required. There are also some suggestions for creating a Parent Skill Questionnaire and a New Parent Pack.

- **PTA cake stall** paper plate idea: some PTAs have found sending out a paper plate with the following rhyme written on it has increased the amount of donations they receive for cake stalls-
    - "I'm a little plate
      As lonely as can be
      Please won't you bake some cakes
      To place upon me?"
      Please bring in your cakes on.....

-Mothers / Fathers Day / Christmas Room

Mothers Day Gift Shop

The PTA are running a Mothers Day Gift Shop for the children on Friday 8th March. This event has been popular with the children over the last few years.

There will be a selection of Mothers Day presents available for the children to choose from. The gift that they choose will be giftwrapped for them to take home to give on Mothers Day.

The cost of the Mothers Day Gift Shop is £2 per child.

Please complete the permission slip below and return it with payment for the Mothers Day Gift Shop via the Bulletin Bag by Monday 4th March. Cheques can be made payable to [insert PTA name here].

Many thanks

The PTA

I give permission for my child(ren) to participate in the Mothers Day Gift Shop and enclose £2 payment per child.

Name of
child(ren):_____

Total payment enclosed: £_____

Parent name and
signature_____

- **Parent skill questionnaire**- suggested questions

You can ask whatever questions you think will give you the information you need. But hopefully the below will help to start writing yours if you haven't done one before:

- o Name and class of child, and contact details of parent
- o What is the best way of contacting you? Are you on social media? Would you be willing to join the PTA's Facebook page so that you can keep up to date with PTA events throughout the year?
- o Have you any particular events that you would be like to attend such as a quiz, summer picnic, Ball, Christmas Fair? Or anything else?
- o Have you been involved with fundraising activities before? If so which organisation(s) did you help and what activity(ies) were you involved with? Would you be willing to help the PTA with fundraising work?
- o Have you any particular skills that you feel the PTA might be able to use? Such as: baking, administration, computers, marketing, social media, printing, painting and decorating, gardening or anything else?
- o Do you work for or own a company that might be willing to support the PTA? Some examples of how a company can support the PTA are:
  - Donating a raffle prize
  - Sponsoring the newsletter or a stall at the Christmas Fair
  - Helping with particular projects such as a garden landscaping company might

be able to assist with improving the children's wildlife garden

- Participating in a match funded scheme for its employees who do fundraising activities for charitable organisations
- Sending staff out on "community days" where they can volunteer to help local good causes with a particular project

- Would you be interested in volunteering to help the PTA with its fundraising activities? We appreciate any and all time that any parent can offer to support us- whether that is just for an hour on a stall at the annual Christmas Fair, or more. Are there any particular fundraising activities you would particularly like to be involved with?
- Would you be interested in helping the PTA to help plan and organise fundraising events- either as a volunteer, class representative or Committee Member?
- Have you any suggestions for fundraising activities that the PTA could consider adding to its programme of fundraising events? Perhaps something that you have helped with or come across elsewhere?
- Is there anything in particular that you would like the PTA to consider funding?
- Any other comments or suggestions

- **New parent pack**

It is a good idea to consider producing an information pack for new parents joining the school. If you can get it to the parents at the induction event even before their children have started at the school, hopefully by the time the new term starts they will have read the pack and will be keen to find out more about the PTA. If you can have a PTA member at the induction event to say a few words to new parents and to give out the induction pack, they will then also have already met a PTA member and hopefully will have had a good first impression of the PTA and the work it does.

Below are some suggestions of what you could include in your new parent pack:

- o Welcome letter from the PTA to all new parents! This could be a nice friendly letter explaining what the PTA is (if it is a registered Charity, you could mention this in the letter), what it does, what it has funded in the last few years, what it is currently fundraising for and how it relies on the continued support of volunteers such as parents to be able to do this. The letter could encourage parents to consider becoming involved and listing the various ways that they can contact the PTA (email / some telephone numbers of willing Committee members / details of the Facebook group etc). You could also mention that joining the PTA will let new parents feel more involved with the school and the activities that their children are doing there.
- o Last PTA newsletter if you do one. This will hopefully give a flavour of the sort of events the PTA runs, and how much money it tends to raise as well as updates on what it has funded.
- o Dates of next few meetings if known.
- o Details of any events that are already planned for the next school year- even if you don't have firm dates you could create a document that tells them about what events the PTA is looking forward to doing in the next school year.
- o New parent questionnaire.

o Easyfundraising flier and accompanying letter
explaining the scheme and encouraging them
to register and start using it straight away. The
letter could mention how much the scheme
has raised to date and give the contact details
of your easyfundraising admin person if they
have any questions about the scheme and
how to use it.

- School disco flier

School Disco!!

The PTA is having a School Disco!! This is open to all children at the school and promises to be great fun for everyone with music to dance to and games to play. There will be prizes to win in the dancing competition!

The School Disco is from 5.30-7.30 p.m. on Friday 6th July. All children will receive a snack and a drink. Dress to impress!

The cost of the School Disco is £2 per child (to include a drink and a snack).

There will also be nail painting and face painting available to children at 50p a go.

Please complete the permission slip below and return it with payment for your child(ren) via the Bulletin Bag by Monday 2nd July.

We look forward to seeing your children there for a fun filled evening!

_____

Name of Child(ren):_____

Payment enclosed (£2 per child): £

Parent name and signature: _____

Please note that the school disco is only available to children who attend the school.

- ## Sample Standing Order mandate for regular parental contributions

---

PTA- Registered Charity Number: 543260

Standing Order Mandate for Donations to the PTA.

Please return to: PTA Treasurer, c/ o School Office, Rotherwood Road, Hitchin.

To: _____ Bank / Building Society

Address:

_____

_____

Please pay: [Insert the PTA's Bank Name, address, sort code] for the credit of PTA account number 126 985

The sum of (in figures) **£_____** (in words)_____

Commencing: _____ and, thereafter, every:_____

Until you receive further notice from me.

Name of account to be debited:

_____

Account number:_____ Sort ode:_____

Signature: _____
Date:_____

- **Sample Gift Aid form**

Gift Aid declaration- Donations

[Insert Name] PTA: Registered Charity Number 543260

Please treat as Gift Aid donations all qualifying gifts of money made from this date.

I confirm that I have paid or will pay an amount of Income Tax and / or Capital Gains Tax for the current tax year (6 April- 5 April) that is at least equal to the amount of tax that all the charities and Community Amateur Sports Clubs (CASCs) that I donate to will reclaim on my gifts for the current tax year. I understand that other taxes such as VAT and Council Tax do not qualify. I understand that the Charity will reclaim 25p of tax on ever £1 that I have given.

Donor's Details:

Title:_____ First Name or Initials: _____

Surname:_____

Full Home
Address:_____

_____Postcode:_____

Signature:_____
Date:_____

---

15 SUPPLIER IDEAS

- **Amazon**- you can buy nearly anything on Amazon. But it is particularly good for sourcing more obscure items like candyfloss machines. It is also on easyfundraising so purchases made on Amazon can earn the PTA cashback via easyfundraising.
- **eBay**- a good source of large quantities of small, inexpensive toys for use in things like Bran Tubs, Lucky Dips and Hook a Duck. Look for Party bag toys. Also with easyfundraising.
- **Engravebricks   Ltd   -   01730   895971** www.engravebricks.co.uk
  Supplier of building bricks that they can engrave with specified names- for use when selling bricks as part of a fundraising drive towards a building project.
- **Fundraising Creations** – www.fundraisingcreations.co.uk
  Supplier of a wide selection of items that can have childrens art work put onto them. There are quite a few companies that will do this so shop around, but this is a good one to look at to start with.
- **Hiscox insurance www.hiscox.co.uk**
  Will provide public liability insurance for holding a dog show in conjunction with the Kennel Club
- **Home Bargains- www.homebargains.co.uk**
  A good source of cheap things to use as Mothers / Fathers Day gifts / Santas Grotto presents and lots of other things. Sadly not on easyfundraising but its prices still make it worth looking at and most items available online.

- **School Recording Stars** – 01282 456450
www.schoolrecordingstars.com
Company who will come and record the children singing songs and create a CD from the recording for the PTA to sell to parents.
- **Webb Ivory** www.webbivory.co.uk
Catalogue / online shopping that can earn the PTA cashback on purchases made by parents
- **Wizard Video** http://wizardvideo.co.uk
Will come and film your school performances for free subject to a minimum order of DVDs sold at £18.95 each (varies with day of the week and number of cameras used). Can also arrange duplication of filming done by parents.
- **Yellow Moon** www.yellowmoon.org.uk
Does a fundraising scheme for PTAs and other good causes. The PTA registers with the scheme and then publicise the scheme in order to encourage parents to order online. The PTA earns commission on any orders that are placed through its registration with the scheme.
- **SOS Charity Fashion Shows**
http://charityfashionshows.co.uk
Will do charity fashion shows for charitable organisations as fundraising events. Good website to look at initially to find out more about how charity fashion shows work, even if they don't cover your area.

16 COMPANIES THAT HAVE MATCH FUNDING SCHEMES

Please note that this is not an exhaustive list- if a parent thinks that their company may offer a match funding scheme, ask them to contact their HR department to find out if they operate one. Also please note that parents who work at companies listed here should also contact their HR to check that the scheme is still running as companies do change their policies. If a company is found to be operating a match funding scheme, further information should be obtained from the company to clarify how their scheme is operated and to confirm that the PTA is eligible to be considered by their scheme for a donation.

3i	Abbey National plc	ABN Amro Bank	Accenture
Alfred Dunhill Ltd.	Alliance and Leicester plc.	Alliance Capital Ltd.	American Express
Amoco Foundation Inc	Anderson	Anglian Water	Argos plc
ARM Holdings	ASDA	AstraZeneca	AT Kearney
BAA plc	Bank of America	Bank of England	Bank of Scotland (HBOS)
Bank of	Bankers Trust	Barclays Bank plc	Barclays

Toyko-Mitsubishi			Capital
Barclays Group / Wealth	Beaverbrooks (Jewellers)	Bell Atlantic Network Services	BG Group
Boeing Commercial Airplanes	Boston Consulting Group	BP Amoco plc. BP Chemicals Ltd.	BP
BP Exploration and Operating Co Ltd.	BP Oil International Ltd.	Bradford and Bingley plc.	Bristol-Myers-Squibb
British American Tobacco	British Army	British Gas	BT
Cable & Wireless	Camelot Group	CapGemini	Capital International Research
Celanese Canada Inc	Centrica plc	Citibank Group	Chase Manhattan Foundation
Citibank	Citigroup	Clifford Chance	Coutts & Co
Credit Suisse First Boston	De La Rue	Deloitte Consulting	Deutsche Bank

DHL	DHL International (UK) Ltd	Diageo	Dixons Group
Dresdner Kleinwort Wasserstein	Eli Lily	EMI	Energis
Ericsson Telecom	Ernst & Young	Experian Ltd	Exxon Mobile
Fidelity Brokerage Services	Fidelity Investments	First Bus	Firstgroup plc.
Ford Motor Company	Gap	GlaxoSmithKline plc	Goldman Sachs
Guardian Royal Exchange plc	Halifax (HBOS)	HSBC	IBM
IDEO	Industrial Bank of Japan	Innogy Plc	Invensys
Kingfisher plc	KPMG	Littlewoods Organisation	Lloyds TSB
Marks and Spencer plc	McKinsey & Co	Mercury Asset Management	Merril Lynch
Microsoft	Midlands Electricity	Mitsubishi Research Institute	Mitsubishi Chemical Corp
Moodys	Morgan	Morgan Stanley Dean	National

Investors Services Ltd	Grenfell	Witter	Power
National Westminster Bank plc (Natwest)	NCR Corporation	NFC	Northern Electric
Pearson	Pfizer	Philip Morris / Philip Morris Companies inc	Philips
Phoenix Home Life Mutual Insurance	PPG Industries Foundation	PricewaterhouseCoopers	Proctor & Gamble
Reuters	Robert Fleming & Co (JP Morgan)	Rolls Royce	Royal and Sun Alliance
Royal Bank of Scotland	Schroders plc	Scottish and Newcastle Brewery	Scottish and Southern Energy
Seaboard	Shell	Siemens Medical	Sigma Securities
SIT Investment Associates Foundation	Sky Broadcasting	Slaughter & May	SmithKline Beecham
Southern Electric	Stagecoach Holdings plc	Standard & Poors	Sun Life of Canada

PTA Fundraising

Swiss Bank Corp	Tesco plc	Texaco	Thames Water
The Economist Group	JP Morgan Chase Foundation	Lloyds TSB Foundation for England and Wales	UBS Warburg
United Airlines	United News and Media	Vodafone	Warner Music
William M Mercer	Wood Group	Yorkshire Water	

Anne Dunn

ABOUT THE AUTHOR

The author has been heavily involved with PTAs for nearly ten years. This included a four year term as Treasurer as well as time doing the work of the Secretary and Chair roles. This has given extensive experience of the mechanics of fundraising events for the PTA. The author has a real understanding challenges that PTAs can face in terms of engagement with parents and finding and keeping volunteers.

Printed in Great Britain
by Amazon